"Given the size and complexity of the bo[c] various candidates for the main theologic[how they all fit together. In this engaging [the idea of God as Trinity is foundational [Luke's other emphases develop and cohere in light of this central truth. This study would be an excellent resource for anyone wishing to delve more deeply into the message and intention of Acts."

David Peterson, Emeritus Faculty Member, Moore College; author, *The Acts of the Apostles*

"Patrick Schreiner offers here a valuable and beautifully wrapped gift to every serious reader of the book of Acts. Not only does Schreiner discuss each major theological theme of Acts in depth, which is itself a significant contribution, but he is careful to show how Luke integrates these various themes into an overarching, powerful, and rich theological message that resonates with the church in every age as it desperately seeks renewal. Schreiner's lively writing style makes this book a joy to read, his many graphs and images render the work easily understandable, and his allusions to contemporary popular culture reinforce his underlying conviction that the message of Acts is every bit as relevant today as when it first burst onto the scene."

David R. Bauer, Ralph Waldo Beeson Professor of Inductive Biblical Studies; Dean, School of Biblical Interpretation, Asbury Theological Seminary

"Patrick Schreiner has given us a solid look at the theology of one of the most underappreciated books of the New Testament: the book of Acts. He shows clearly how Luke's look at history and the promise that is at the heart of the early church is not about the acts of the apostles but about the unfolding acts of God that are still at work in our world. This work will develop your appreciation for what God has done and is doing, and who we are called to be as members of his church."

Darrell L. Bock, Executive Director of Cultural Engagement, The Hendricks Center, Dallas Theological Seminary

The Mission of the Triune God

New Testament Theology

Edited by Thomas R. Schreiner and Brian S. Rosner

The Mission of the Triune God: A Theology of Acts, Patrick Schreiner

The Joy of Hearing: A Theology of the Book of Revelation, Thomas R. Schreiner

The Mission of the Triune God

A Theology of Acts

Patrick Schreiner

WHEATON, ILLINOIS

Library of Congress Cataloging-in-Publication Data

Names: Schreiner, Patrick, author.
Title: The mission of the triune God : a theology of Acts / Patrick Schreiner.
Description: Wheaton, Illinois : Crossway, [2022] | Series: New Testament theology | Includes bibliographical references and index.
Identifiers: LCCN 2021014184 (print) | LCCN 2021014185 (ebook) | ISBN 9781433574115 (trade paperback) | ISBN 9781433574122 (pdf) | ISBN 9781433574139 (mobipocket) | ISBN 9781433574146 (epub)
Subjects: LCSH: Bible. Acts—Theology.
Classification: LCC BS2625.52 .S365 2022 (print) | LCC BS2625.52 (ebook) | DDC 226.6/06—dc23
LC record available at https://lccn.loc.gov/2021014184
LC ebook record available at https://lccn.loc.gov/2021014185

To Hannah—
My coworker in this mission.

Contents

Illustrations

Tables

Figures

Series Preface

THERE ARE REMARKABLY FEW treatments of the big ideas of single books of the New Testament. Readers can find brief coverage in Bible dictionaries, in some commentaries, and in New Testament theologies, but such books are filled with other information and are not devoted to unpacking the theology of each New Testament book in its own right. Technical works concentrating on various themes of New Testament theology often have a narrow focus, treating some aspect of the teaching of, say, Matthew or Hebrews in isolation from the rest of the book's theology.

The New Testament Theology series seeks to fill this gap by providing students of Scripture with readable book-length treatments of the distinctive teaching of each New Testament book or collection of books. The volumes approach the text from the perspective of biblical theology. They pay due attention to the historical and literary dimensions of the text, but their main focus is on presenting the teaching of particular New Testament books about God and his relations to the world on their own terms, maintaining sight of the Bible's overarching narrative and Christocentric focus. Such biblical theology is of fundamental importance to biblical and expository preaching and informs exegesis, systematic theology, and Christian ethics.

The twenty volumes in the series supply comprehensive, scholarly, and accessible treatments of theological themes from an evangelical perspective. We envision them being of value to students, preachers, and interested laypeople. When preparing an expository sermon series, for example, pastors can find a healthy supply of informative commentaries, but there are few options for coming to terms with the overall teaching of each book of the New Testament. As well as being useful in sermon and Bible study preparation, the volumes will also be of value as textbooks in college and seminary exegesis classes. Our prayer is that they contribute to a deeper understanding of and commitment to the kingdom and glory of God in Christ.

Patrick Schreiner's Acts volume, *The Mission of the Triune God*, lays out in engaging style the theology of a unique book in the New Testament. The book of Acts bridges the gap between the Gospels and the Epistles and recounts the birth of the church age. But too often its theology, presented in narrative form, goes untapped. Schreiner reads Acts as a programmatic document, calling on and equipping the church to press on with the task of witness to the end of the earth. Acts is about resurrection life, the expansion of the temple of the Lord, and the advance of the word of the Lord. It has a high view of Jesus Christ and the Holy Spirit, and also a high view of the church as central to God's purposes. Delightfully punctuated with appropriate popular culture references, *The Mission of the Triune God* is an eminently practical as well as profound presentation of the main themes of Acts.

Thomas R. Schreiner and Brian S. Rosner

Preface

EVERY BOOK I STUDY IN THE BIBLE becomes my new favorite. That is currently the case with Acts. Spending significant time in any part of Scripture allows one to see the breadth, depth, and beauty of the words from God himself. As Gregory the Great once said, Scripture is shallow enough for a child to play in but deep enough for an elephant to drown in.[1] I like to become an elephant, minus the drowning.

This book is a biblical theology of Acts. Biblical theology can be done in a variety of ways. The work in your hands does not trace the narrative of Acts so much as follow the *theological themes* through *narrative order* (cf. Luke 1:3). It is a logically and narratively ordered treatment of the major theological themes in Acts.

The outline came to me when I was working on my commentary on Acts in the Christian Standard Commentary Series (2022). Some of that material is reproduced, reorganized, and expanded here. Sections of chapter 2 also stem from my thoughts in *The Ascension of Christ* with Lexham Press (2020). I am thankful to both publishers for allowing me to reproduce some of the material here.[2]

---

1 Gregory the Great, "Letter to Leander," in *Moral Reflections on the Book of Job*, trans. Brian Kerns (Collegeville, MN: Liturgical Press; Athens, OH: Cistercian Publications, 2014), 53: "It has out in the open food for children but keeps hidden away the things that fill the minds of the eminent with awe. Scripture is like a river again, broad and deep, shallow enough here for the lamb to go wading, but deep enough there for the elephant to swim."

2 Patrick Schreiner, *Acts*, Christian Standard Commentary (Nashville, TN: Holman, 2022); *The Ascension of Christ: Recovering a Neglected Doctrine* (Bellingham, WA: Lexham, 2020).

My prayer is you will see that the many themes of Acts do not compete with one another but work in harmony. Acts has a Trinitarian shape, and God has a mission to accomplish. Or to put it another way, the Father has a plan for his people, which centers on the exalted Son and goes forth by the empowering Spirit. From this Trinitarian river all other themes flow, like water from the temple renewing God's church in every age.

The soundtrack for this book came mainly from Jon Guerra's album *Keeper of Days*. It released after I was done with two chapters and became my go-to album for the rest of the chapters. I also consistently listened to the soundtrack of the movie *A Hidden Life*, with the score by James Newton Howard. The newest Lone Bellow album, *Half Moon Light,* also snuck its way into my playlist.

Because the Scriptures have a musical quality, and because the Father's plan can also be described as his "orchestration," I have capitalized on the musical theme and begin many chapters with a musical illustration.

Thanks to the many friends who read this book before it was published and who pointed out many mistakes and unclear sentences. Chad Ashby caught numerous errors, and I can't give him enough credit. Nathan Ridlehoover read pieces of the book and gave helpful suggestions. Julia Mayo pointed out a few places where I needed to change wording.

Thank you to the series editors, Brian Rosner and Tom Schreiner, for inviting me to be a part of this series. I know Tom somewhat, and Brian is a swell scholar. All other mistakes should be attributed to Voldemort.

Abbreviations

Ant.	Josephus, *Antiquities*
BBR	*Bulletin for Biblical Research*
BECNT	Baker Exegetical Commentary on the New Testament
Il.	Homer, *Illiad*
INT	*Interpretation*
JBL	*Journal of Biblical Literature*
JECH	*Journal of Early Christian History*
JETS	*Journal of the Evangelical Theological Society*
JSNT	*Journal for the Study of the New Testament*
JSNTSS	*Journal for the Study of New Testament Supplmental Series*
JTS	*Journal of Theological Studies*
LNTS	Library of New Testament Studies
NIDNTTE	New International Dictionary of New Testament Theology and Exegesis
NPNF	*Nicene and Post-Nicene Fathers*
NSBT	New Studies in Biblical Theology
NTS	*New Testament Studies*
PNTC	Pillar New Testament Commentary
PTMS	Princeton Theological Monograph Series
SNTSMS	Society for New Testament Studies Monograph Series
TDNT	*Theological Dictionary of the New Testament*

Introduction

Acts as a Renewal Document

The Uniqueness of Acts

The book of Acts offers something unique in the Christian canon. It has no rival in terms of a book spanning so many different lands. Its references to the Spirit far outpace any other work. It functions as a hinge canonically, bridging the Gospels and Epistles. It recounts the birth of the church age. And its content has no parallel in the New Testament.

Some of Paul's letters correspond to each other, and the four Gospels overlap, but most of what is found in Acts can be found in no other document. Without Acts, there would be no account of fire and wind at Pentecost. No description of Peter's encounter with Cornelius. No narrative of the rise of the multiethnic church in Antioch. No story of Paul's visit to Philippi, Corinth, or Ephesus, or of Paul's trials in Jerusalem and Caesarea.

Acts is also unique in that it might be our only writing from a Gentile—in addition to the Gospel by Luke. Colossians 4:11–14 gives a strong, but not decisive, argument for Luke's Gentile status, since Paul lists Luke after those of the circumcision party.

The New Testament is largely written to deal with the Jew and Gentile dispute in light of Jesus's arrival. If this is what the New Testament concerns, then it is remarkable that 27 percent of the

New Testament (Luke-Acts) comes from a Gentile mind, heart, and quill.[1]

Acts is also unparalleled in that it recounts a new stage in Christian history: post-Jesus life. Everything (canonically) before this has been either pre-Jesus or with-Jesus. No longer are readers or characters looking forward to a Messiah, or following him on the dusty roads of Galilee. Now readers get a glimpse of Jesus's followers as they seek to be faithful to Jesus after he has departed.

The new community must figure out how to act now that Christ is gone. What has God instructed them to do? Where is the kingdom? How will they respond to persecution and pressures? What is the future of God's people? How do they live under the rule of Rome as a marginal and contested community?

Acts, as a unique part of the canon, coming from a distinctive voice, lays out the unparalleled story of the early church to encourage the church to press on. It therefore has much to say to the church in every generation. As Erasmus wrote to Pope Clement VII in 1524, Acts presents "the foundations of the newborn church . . . through [which] we hope that the church in ruins will be reborn."[2]

In other words, Acts is a model, a prototype, an exemplar for the renewal of the church. Luke, as a travel companion of Paul, kept his eye on the community of faith and so should any modern reading of Acts. This story is for more than the people of God, but aimed primarily to encourage God's people.

---

1   A few early Christians also identify Luke as from Antioch. The Anti-Marcionite Prologue (end of second century; cf. "Anti-Marcionite [Gospel] Prologues," in *Anchor Bible Dictionary*, vol. 1, ed. David Noel Freedman [New York: Doubleday, 1992], 262) describes Luke as "an Antiochene of Syria." Some even argue "Lucius of Cyrene" in Acts 13:1 is Luke (cf. Rom. 16:21). If he is from Cyrene, the north coast of Africa, then he likely had dark skin. Though this is hard to confirm, if true, Luke-Acts is the only work authored by a black Gentile. While many modern scholars doubt this, as Paul elsewhere calls him Luke (Col. 4:14; 2 Tim. 4:11; Philem. 24), it should be taken into account that the two most "Roman" books (Romans and Acts) call some obscure figure Lucius.

2   Desiderius Erasmus, *Paraphrase on Acts*, trans. Robert D. Sider, vol. 50 of *Collected Works of Erasmus* (Toronto: University of Toronto Press, 1995), 4.

Acts speaks to the church in two different ways: as a *transitional* and a *programmatic* book.[3] As a *transitional* book, Acts recounts nonrepeatable events that establish the community of faith. For example, Pentecost is an unrepeatable event, but also not retractable. The reestablishment of the twelve apostles is exclusive to the period of Acts. The fate of Ananias and Sapphira is not likely to be seen requiring the immediate termination of liars in the church today.

However, Acts also confronts Christians as a *programmatic book*. It provides guidance for the church in every age. Its message can't be locked in the past. Its accomplishments can't be relegated to a bygone era. Its miracles can't be separated to another age. The same Spirit is still active. The same Christ still rules. The same God still sustains his church. The same resurrection days reside.

The scope of what happens in Acts is nothing short of remarkable. Within the space of thirty years, the gospel is preached in the most splendid, formidable, and corrupt cities.[4] It reaches the Holy City (Jerusalem), the City of Philosophers (Athens), the City of Magic (Ephesus), and the Empire (Rome). Its message and work were not done in a corner. Its victories and opposition were not minor blips in history. Acts recounts the struggle and success of the gospel message going forth, all under the plan of God, centered on King Jesus, and empowered by the Spirit.

The triumph of this movement cannot be attributed to the apostles or Paul but only to God himself. The change brought about by the twelve apostles is the most inexplicable, mysterious, and wonderful event ever witnessed in this world. Luke writes to encourage the church, telling it *this* is the plan of God. His kingdom plan is not put on hiatus once Christ leaves; rather, it kicks into higher gear as the Spirit comes and the good news goes to Jerusalem, Judea and Samaria, and finally to the ends of the earth (1:8).

---

3   I borrow this language from Brandon D. Crowe, *The Hope of Israel: The Resurrection of Christ in the Acts of the Apostles* (Grand Rapids, MI: Baker Academic, 2020), 4.

4   The next two paragraphs are a reworking and paraphrasing of Barnes's moving summary of Acts. Albert Barnes, *Notes Explanatory and Practical on the Acts of the Apostles* (New York: Harper, 1851), vi.

The Purpose of Acts: Assurance

The purposes of Acts are bound up in the narrative rather than in abstractions. It is fruitless to try to boil Luke's story down to one purpose. Surely, Acts is a multilayered and multipurposed document.[5] In addition, Spirit-inspired literature such as this outlives its immediate purposes to instruct and challenge future generations, even in ways the human author could not completely foresee.

Having said all that, it is still beneficial to ascertain some key and fundamental purposes for Acts. Luke is the only writer in the New Testament to give us a prescript for both of his volumes (Luke 1:1–4; Acts 1:1–5), which ends up being extremely helpful for determining his purpose. Luke's preface for his Gospel is as follows:

> Since many have attempted to organize a *narrative* of the deeds that have been *fulfilled* among us, just as those who from the beginning were eyewitnesses and ministers of the word have delivered them to us, it seemed good to me also, having followed all things closely for some time past, to write an *orderly sequence* for you, most excellent Theophilus, that you may *know* with *certainty* concerning the things you have been taught. (Luke 1:1–4, my translation)

The purposes orbit around these italicized words: narrative—fulfilled—orderly—know—certainty. The narrative itself, the ordering, provides certainty about the fulfillment of God's promises. But what was this uncertainty and what was fulfilled?

Interestingly, Luke employs the same language (*know* and *certainty*) and concepts (*fulfill*) of Luke 1:4 again in Acts 2:36. At the end of Peter's Pentecost sermon, he tells the crowd, "Let all the house of Israel *know* with *certainty* that God has made this Jesus, whom you crucified, both Lord and Messiah" (2:36, my translation).[6]

---

5   Mark Powell categorizes the proposals for a purpose of Acts under six headings: irenic, polemical, apologetic, evangelistic, pastoral, and theological. Mark Allan Powell, *What Are They Saying about Acts?* (New York: Paulist, 1991), 13–19.

6   The same word for certainty resurfaces once more in the judicial contexts of Acts where Paul argues Jesus is the Messiah (21:34; 22:30; 25:26).

Thus, Luke provides *certainty through an ordered narrative* that God has *fulfilled* his promises to Israel and the nations *in* Jesus Christ.[7] He writes an arranged story to show Jesus and the Spirit are the Father's plan for his people—both now and forevermore. In this way, Acts is a work of edification; it has a *theological* and *pastoral* purpose for local communities.[8] As Craig Keener states, "Luke's largest agenda in Luke-Acts is to place the mission of Jesus and the church in its place in salvation history."[9]

At the highest level, Luke writes to convince his audience that the bumpy start of the community of God *is* the plan of God. Luke's audience needs *assurance* that they are on the right path. As the church endures rejection and persecution, God's people might not be sure this is the fulfillment of the kingdom.

In many ways, Acts can be seen as a series of onslaughts of Satan trying to thwart the spread of the word. Ironically, the onslaughts only propel it forward. Luke, therefore, reassures Christians of the nature and plan of God. This is the primary purpose of Acts.

However, many subcategories exist below this larger purpose. If Luke wrote to provide theological and pastoral certainty, then the uncertainty he counters can be identified with even more precision. This uncertainty seems to have stemmed from ethnic, gender, supernatural, social, economic, and political realities. All of these created pressure points, persecution, or disunity.[10]

---

7   The word translated "orderly" (*kathexēs*) doesn't so much mean chronological but refers to a logical and coherent sequence (cf. Luke 8:1; Acts 3:24; 18:23).

8   Howard Marshall also claims Acts was intended as "an account of Christian beginnings in order to strengthen faith and give assurance that its foundation is sure." I. Howard Marshall, *The Acts of the Apostles: An Introduction and Commentary* (Grand Rapids, MI: Eerdmans, 1980), 21.

9   Craig S. Keener, *Acts: An Exegetical Commentary*, vol. 1, *Introduction and 1:1–2:47* (Grand Rapids, MI: Baker Academic, 2012), 438.

10 As Philip Esler notes, the actual condition of Luke's community governs his theology. He has molded his work to minister to the needs of the community and therefore gives modern ministers the impetus to stay attuned to the social, economic, and political realities of our own time. Philip Francis Esler, *Community and Gospel in Luke-Acts* (Cambridge: Cambridge University Press, 1987), 223.

Ethnically, the new community now consisted of both Jews and Gentiles, which caused problems. Jews wondered whether welcoming Gentiles to table-fellowship necessarily implied the abandonment of their ancestral faith.

Politically, Gentiles wondered how they fit into a religious movement that had its roots in Judaism, and all Christians pondered how their newfound faith inhabited the Empire.

Socially, this community consisted of both rich and poor, and the culture of the day had a wide separation of the two groups.

In terms of *gender*, women were a large contingent of the early church, and Luke wrote to affirm the diversity.

Supernaturally, this community was under attack by demonic forces and the power of Satan.

Figure 1.1   Uncertainty in Acts

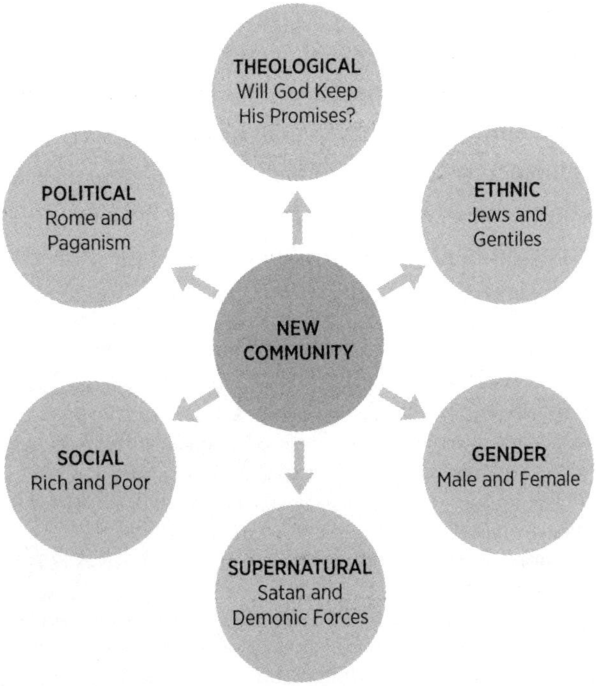

Luke, therefore, shows readers through his ordered narrative that Jews and Gentiles are to engage in table-fellowship together; Christianity fulfills ancestral Judaism; the gospel is for the rich and the poor; the rich are to provide for the poor; Christianity and Rome don't have to be at odds; the Way is innocent of sedition against Caesar; both women and men are welcome in the church; and the Satanic and political forces have no power over the message of Christ.

Furthermore, Luke tells these stories so the future church can emulate the virtuous acts and avoid the shameful ones. Literature in the ancient world presented its subjects as exemplars to instruct and inform concerning the current moment.

All of the above points combine to form a theological, pastoral, historical, evangelistic, and even political purpose.[11] *Luke writes to encourage, to embolden emulation, and to evangelize.* It is a renewal document for all times.

The Plan and Argument

The rest of this book will outline the ordered narrative theology of Acts. God imparts a theology in Acts for the renewal of the church. Yet the proposals for a theological center or theological heart of Acts twist in a variety of directions.

Many claim Acts focuses on the Spirit. The Spirit is thus the primary actor in Acts, making this the "Acts of the Holy Spirit." Others claim it is the word, which becomes almost a character in Acts with arms and legs. Others claim it is the church. Acts exists to teach us about the struggles of the early church. Others claim Acts is about the transition from Peter to Paul—after all, this is the *Acts of the Apostles.* More recent proposals focus on the continued work of Jesus.

---

11   F. F. Bruce says Luke is an apologist in Acts: he defends Christianity against pagan religion (Christianity is true, paganism is false), against Judaism (Christianity is the fulfillment of true Judaism), and against political accusations (Christianity is innocent of any offence against Roman law). F. F. Bruce, *The Acts of the Apostles,* 3rd rev. and enlarged ed. (Grand Rapids, MI: Eerdmans, 1990), 22.

Elements of truth persist in each of these proposals. But rather than claiming one outdoes the others, it is better to recognize they all relate to one another. Coherency and association rather than conflict and antagonism unite these themes together. Too many propose a different central theme, arguing past one another, not realizing they are arguing for the same thing but from a different angle.

Benefit, therefore, exists in locating these themes in a logical and conceptual order. Rather than being disparate, these themes are a mosaic—the pieces fit together. To put them out of place does damage to our understanding as a whole.

The order, to no surprise, is found in Luke's narrative (cf. Luke 1:3). To put this another way, one cannot theologize Acts correctly without *narratizing* it. As Richard Pervo puts it, "Acts is a narrative, and its theology must be recovered from the narrative."[12]

For example, one can't speak about the Spirit according to Acts without putting him in the frame of the risen Christ. One can't speak of Christ without speaking of the Father's plan. One can't speak about the witness of the apostles without relating it to the empowering of the Spirit. This book is most fundamentally about the mission of the triune God.

I have chosen seven themes to summarize Luke's main theological aims, though certainly many more could be added: (1) *God the Father* orchestrates; (2) through *Christ*, who lives and rules; and (3) through the empowering *Spirit*; (4) causing the *word* to multiply; (5) bringing *salvation* to all; (6) forming the *church*; which (7) *witnesses* to the ends of the earth.

Luke emphasizes all of these themes in different ways, but my order is purposeful—a Lukan logic exists. The triune God stands at the head because the remaining themes flow from God the Father's plan, centered on the risen and enthroned Jesus, and the empowerment of the Spirit. The Spirit then empowers *the word* concerning salvation in Jesus's name. Through the word, *salvation* in Jesus's name is announced to all

---

12   Richard Pervo, *Acts: A Commentary*, Hermeneia (Minneapolis, MN: Fortress, 2008), 22.

flesh. Salvation creates *the church* (the body of Christ), which *witnesses* to the actions of the triune God.

When all of these are tied together, the priority of the Trinitarian shape surfaces from the message of Acts. Acts is about God, the God who continues his mission to glorify himself by blessing the nations through his chosen people. Though this book is about God, the agency of God never negates the agency of his people; it empowers them. The time has come to look at each of these theological themes in more detail for the renewal of the church.

Figure 1.2   Theological Themes in Acts

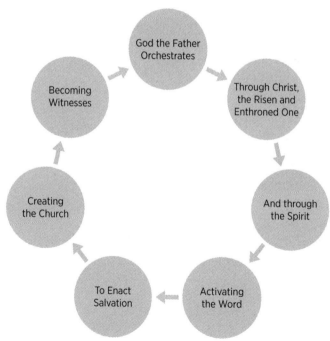

- God the Father Orchestrates
- Through Christ, the Risen and Enthroned One
- And through the Spirit
- Activating the Word
- To Enact Salvation
- Creating the Church
- Becoming Witnesses

1

God the Father Orchestrates

For if this plan or this undertaking is of man, it will fail;
but if it is of God, you will not be able to overthrow them.

ACTS 5:38–39

The Father and the Ensemble

One of my favorite classical songs is Gustav Holst's "Jupiter, the Bringer of Jolity." A long time ago, I found a YouTube video of "Jupiter" performed by the Osaka Philharmonic Orchestra with Eiji Oue as the conductor. He likely spent countless hours on this project, working through the mistakes, the mistimings, and mismanagement.

Midway through the song, the string section arises in full force. Oue's face fills with emotion as he directs them to be one with their instruments and one another. He conducts a masterpiece. He guides the song to its natural, prewritten, and beautiful end.[1]

If Acts is a song, then the Father conducts the ensemble. Similar to Oue, God the Father orchestrates all actions in Acts toward their prewritten and beautiful end. He has a plan. And it will be accomplished.

---

1   My wife and I love the song so much that we used the strings portion for her walk down the aisle at our wedding.

Though most theological works on Acts don't begin with the Father (and sometimes don't even include him in one of the themes), it is clear throughout the narrative that all the action finds its source *in* and stems *from* the Father.[2]

All other refrains in Acts flow from the Father's orchestration. Acts *is* about Christ, the Spirit, and the church, but these—to use early church language—are begotten from, spirate from, and are born from God the Father. A theology of Acts must start with the Father, his plan and orchestration.

It is the Father who acts (2:11; 14:27; 15:4, 7–8, 14; 21:19); speaks (2:17; 3:21; 7:6–7; 8:14); attests to Jesus (2:22); raised Jesus from the dead (2:24; 3:15, 22, 26; 4:10; 5:30; 7:37; 10:40; 13:30, 37; 26:8); anointed Jesus (10:38); appointed him to be judge (10:42); swore an oath to David (2:30); is seated in the heavens (2:33; 7:56); made Jesus Lord, Messiah, Leader, and Savior (2:36; 5:31); calls people (2:39); deserves worship (2:47; 3:8–9; 4:21; 16:25; 18:7, 13; 22:3; 23:1; 24:14–16); is the God of Israel's ancestors (3:13, 25; 7:17, 32, 46; 13:17; 22:14); fulfilled what he said in the Scriptures (3:18; 13:33); deserves obedience (4:19; 5:4, 29; 10:4); listens (4:24); reveals (4:31; 6:7; 10:28; 12:24); orchestrates (5:39; 10:15); delivers (7:25, 35, 45); punishes (7:42; 12:23); has power (8:10); gave the Holy Spirit (5:32; 8:20; 11:17); is glorious (7:2, 55; 11:18), great (10:46), gracious (11:23; 13:43; 14:26; 27:24), present (7:9; 10:33), and alive (14:15); helps (26:22); doesn't show favoritism (10:34); appoints witnesses (10:41); is to be feared (13:16, 26); performs wonders (15:12; 19:11); calls (16:10); created all things (17:24); commands (17:30); demands repentance (20:21); deserves thanks (27:35; 28:15); has a plan (20:27); establishes a church (20:28); and provides salvation (28:28).

Darrell Bock rightly declares, "God is the major actor in Luke-Acts," and Squires concludes the plan of God "functions as the foundational theological motif" for Luke-Acts.[3]

2   Bock and Squires are notable exceptions. Darrell L. Bock, *A Theology of Luke and Acts: God's Promised Program, Realized for All Nations*, ed. Andreas J. Köstenberger (Grand Rapids, MI: Zondervan, 2012); John T. Squires, *The Plan of God in Luke-Acts*, SNTSMS 76 (Cambridge: Cambridge University Press, 1993).

3   Bock, *A Theology of Luke and Acts*, 99; John Squires, "The Plan of God in the Acts of the Apostles," in *Witness to the Gospel: The Theology of Acts*, ed. I. Howard Marshall and

While many focus on the earthly sphere, everything in Acts moves according to the heavenly scepter. Luke's principal theological, philosophical, logical, geographical compass is the heavens. All earthly action has prior orchestration and plan.

This chapter will cover the Father's orchestration in three parts. First, I will look at the plan of God, then the word of God, and finally at the kingdom of God.[4] As Rosner summarizes,

> The message in Acts is described as the "word of God" (see Luke 3:2–17; 5:1; 8:11; Acts 4:29, 31; 6:2, 7; 8:14; 11:1; 12:24; 13:5, 7, 44, 46, 48; 16:32; 17:13; 18:11), its content concerns "the kingdom of God" (1:3; 8:12; 14:22; 19:8; 28:23, 31) and "the salvation of God" (28:28; cf., 7:25), and its progress depends upon the "purpose," "will" and "plan" of God.[5]

However, complementing Rosner, I will focus on the word not only as a message but also as an *agent*. God is the conductor, whose agent is the word (orchestra), and the music is the kingdom ("Jupiter").[6] To put it in the frame of Genesis, God's creative will is performed by his word, which brings life (the kingdom). This is the song God has been directing from the beginning of time.

Table 1.1   The Father Orchestrates

Concept	Logical Relationship	Orchestra Analogy
The Plan of God	Purpose	Conductor
The Word of God	Agent	Orchestra
The Kingdom of God	Content	Performance

David Peterson (Grand Rapids, MI: Eerdmans, 1998), 23. For the detailed discussion, see Squires, *The Plan of God in Luke-Acts.*

4 I will spend the most time on the first point (the plan of God), as subsequent chapters will deal with the other themes.

5 Brian Rosner, "The Progress of the Word," in Howard and Peterson, *Witness to the Gospel*, 224.

6 Or, to change the metaphor to a governmental analogy, God is the administrator (Bartlett), the word is his press secretary (C. J. Craig) and the content is the briefing (Toby). Let the reader understand. Other "agents" will be discussed in later chapters.

The Plan of God

Luke arranges the story of the early church in the broadest possible theological context: the plan of God.[7] He begins his two volumes by speaking of "events that have been fulfilled among us" (Luke 1:1 CSB) pointing to the plan of God behind it all. Enhancing this picture is Luke's use of terms such as "plan," "foreknown," "foretold," "predestined," "promised," "ordained," or "worked" through God's choice.[8]

Boulē *in Acts*

Every theme is somehow connected to the Father's plan (*boulē*), and thus Luke employs this term as a theological ballast. The Father's plan can be seen by Luke's emphasis on the activity of the Son and Spirit, manifestations of divine agents, and even miracles. Human characters are subsidiary to the larger story of divine activity.[9]

The word *boulē* is a political and governmental term employed in cities of the Empire.[10] It was a management expression, an administration of a *polis* led by some governmental official. The Father's plan in Acts is to fulfill his promises by creating his new community that will bless the world.

The Father's agents are the Son and Spirit. Peter specifically uses the word *boulē* to speak of God's "appointed or 'definite plan'" in terms of Jesus's being delivered up to death (Acts 2:23). God's plan is centered on Jesus's passion and glorification. Jesus creates a new people and brings about a new era.[11]

---

7   See Squires, "The Plan of God."
8   Bock, *A Theology of Luke and Acts*, 125.
9   Beverly R. Gaventa, *Acts*, Abingdon New Testament Commentaries (Nashville, TN: Abingdon, 2003), 27.
10   NIDNTTE, ed. Moises Silva (Grand Rapids, MI: Zondervan, 2014), 1:256, says, "The noun *boulē* means 'will' and, more strongly, 'determination,' but it freq. carries the sense 'counsel, advice' and can be applied to a deliberative body or 'council' (Homer *Il.* 2.53)." A local city typically had a state council (*boulē*), a male citizen body (*dēmos*), divided into tribes (*phylē*), comprising the state assembly (*ekklēsia*).
11   The plan of God is focused on Jesus. In Isaiah 9:5 it says a child to be born will be a wonderful "counselor" (*boulēs*). Isaiah 11:2 states the Spirit of "counsel" (*boulēs*) will rest upon the anointed figure. See also Ps. 33:10–11; Mic. 4:2.

Then Jesus himself announces this new era when he appears to his disciples after his suffering to tell them the plan is on track. The next phase is about anticipation: they are to wait in Jerusalem for the promise of the Father (Acts 1:4–5; 2:33; cf. Luke 3:16; 24:49). If Acts is about the Holy Spirit, it is first about the Father's promise.

In Acts 2, the plan unfurls as the Spirit falls on God's people. The Father's promise comes to fulfillment as the Spirit is poured out on all flesh (2:17) and the Spirit is then given to Samaritans (8:14–17) and Cornelius (10:44–45), signifying Gentiles are also welcome and thus fulfilling the Lord's words from Acts 1:4 (cf. 11:16).

However, the plan of God for his people that centers on the Son and Spirit does not advance unopposed. Neither earthly nor spiritual powers will comply with the divine decree. Ironically, every effort to thwart only furthers his plan.

A particularly clear example of this comes in Acts 4:23–31 when the apostles gather and pray for boldness after they have been castigated for performing a resurrection miracle. They reflect on this opposition, noting even that this suffering is the *boulē* of God. The people gathered against Jesus "to do whatever your hand and your [*boulē*] had predestined to take place" (4:28).[12] The apostles put the opposition to them under the banner of the *boulē* of God. Persecution is not outside God's will. It is his very design. Jesus already told them many would lay their hands on them, persecute them, and deliver them up to synagogues, prisons, kings, and governors (Luke 21:12).

God's sovereign plan also shines in Gamaliel's speech when the apostles are once more arrested for preaching and healing in Jesus's name (Acts 5:33–42). In 5:38–39, Gamaliel draws his conclusion from the two examples he has given, both of which logically lead to staying away from these men. He says, "If this *boulē* is of human origin, it will fail" (my translation and paraphrase). On the other hand, if it is of God, the temple leaders will not be able to destroy them. Gamaliel says the movement will either be destroyed on its own (because it is

---

12   Both the words in 4:28, "plan" and "predestined," link back to 2:23.

of human origin) or no one will be able to destroy it (because it is the *boulē* of God).

Gamaliel adds one final note indicating the possibility that they may even be found "opposing God" (*theomachoi*), a word that more literally means "God-fighter." Those who oppose God's people and his plan are "God-fighters." Those to whom Luke writes are God-lovers (*theophilus*, 1:1). In Luke's theology, there are two paths: loving God's plan or warring against it.

Fulfillment in Acts

Not only is the plan of God evident in the use of the term *boulē*, but every narrative in Acts, from the smallest to the largest, can be put under the banner of *fulfillment*. This means Luke wrote showing the Father was conducting and orchestrating all the events. For example, in Acts, the large narrative blocks as a whole fulfill the Scripture.[13] Most argue 1:8 functions as the table of contents for Acts:

> But you will receive power when the Holy Spirit has come upon you, and you will be my witnesses in Jerusalem and in all Judea and Samaria, and to the end of the earth.

The rest of Acts details how the apostles and God's people are witnesses in Jerusalem, Judea and Samaria, and Rome. However, many miss the Isaiah echoes packed into this commission (see table 1.2).

Acts, therefore, fulfills Isaianic prophecy. However, as one turns to more detailed narrative analysis, the fulfillment theme continues as the Old Testament Scriptures are either quoted or alluded to. In every section of Acts, evidence exists that God directs this story. God conducts the entire musical score by directing each individual instrument.

---

13 The fulfillment theme can be further seen in the way that the term *dei* (it is necessary) occurs throughout Acts. Luke says it was necessary that Judas defect and be replaced (1:16–20). It is necessary that Jesus ascend (3:21). It is necessary that the apostles be persecuted and obey God rather than man (5:29; 9:16; 14:22). It is necessary for Paul to go to Jerusalem and Rome and Caesar (19:21; 23:11; 27:24). It is even necessary that Paul's ship must run aground on the way to Rome (27:26).

Table 1.2   Fulfillment of Isaianic Prophecy

Acts 1:8	Isaiah
"When the Holy Spirit has come on you"	"Until the Spirit is poured upon us from on high" (32:15)
"You will be my witnesses"	"You are my witnesses" (43:10, 12; 44:8)
"To the end of the earth"	"I will make you as a light for the nations, / that my salvation may reach to the end of the earth" (49:6; cf. 45:22)

Jesus ascends in fulfillment of Psalm 2, Psalm 110:1, and Daniel 7:13–14 (Acts 1:9–11). Both Judas's defection and replacement fulfill the Scriptures (Acts 1:15–26; cf. Pss. 69:25; 109:8). The pouring out of the Spirit fulfills Joel 2:28–32 (Acts 2:1–21). Jesus's resurrection and exaltation completes the hopes for a Messiah (Acts 2:22–36; cf. Pss. 16:8–11; 110:1). The temple restoration scene of the lame man walking and leaping alludes to hopes for a new era (Isa. 35:6; Mic. 4:6–7).

Peter's sermon about the raised servant fulfills the servant theme (Acts 3:11–26; cf. Isa. 52:13–53:12). Even the temple conflict completes the Scriptures as the apostles quote from Psalm 2 (Acts 4:1–31). The generous community embodies the hopes of a new Torah people (Acts 4:32–37; 6:1–7; cf. Deut. 15:4), and even Ananias and Sapphira's death satisfies the fate of those who oppose God and his people (Acts 5:1–11; cf. Lev. 10; Josh. 7). Stephen's temple sermon walks through Abraham, Joseph, Moses, and the entire biblical storyline with an eye on the presence of God (Acts 7:2–53; cf. Isa. 66:1–2).

Acts 8–12 also fulfills the Scriptures. Philip, led by the providence of God, unites Samaria to Jerusalem, fulfilling Ezekiel 37. The eunuch becomes a pillar in God's temple, achieving Isaiah 56:3–8 (Acts 8). Paul is called as a prophet of old and sees Jesus when Ezekiel's vision was obscured as to who was on the throne (Acts 9; cf. Ezek. 1:26–28). Peter realizes God does not show favoritism when he goes into Cornelius's home (Acts 10:34–35; cf. Deut. 10:17–19). Antioch becomes the first multiethnic gathering, realizing Isaiah 55:3–5 (Acts 11:19–30). God sends his witnesses past Jerusalem in fulfillment of a new exodus pattern (Acts 12; cf. Isa. 40:3; 41:18–19; 43:18–19; 48:20; 51:11; 52:11–12).

Acts 13–20 also fulfills the Scriptures. Paul goes to the coasts and islands (Isa. 11:11; 24:15) and proclaims Jesus as a light to the Gentiles (Acts 13:47; cf. Isa 49:6) and the one who rebuilds David's tent (Acts 15:16–17; cf. Amos 9:11–12). Paul declares Jesus fulfills the Scriptures (Acts 13:17–39; 14:3; 17:2–3; 18:5; 19:8), God as the creator of all things (Acts 14:15; 17:24–29), and the arrival of the Spirit (19:3–5), and warns those who will not listen (Acts 13:41; cf. Hab. 1:5).

In the final section of Acts (Acts 21–28), though Paul seems to be caught up in a swirl of events beyond his control, the narrative indicates this is all according to divine plan. Prophecies and visions fill the narrative (20:23; 21:4; 21:11; 23:11) to remind readers, in the midst of the whirlwind, that the divine plan is carried forth (19:21; 20:22–23; 21:11). God's plan is for Paul to witness to kings and Gentiles. The trials fulfill Act 9:15 and Luke 21:12–15 as he testifies before kings. Even Israel's rejection of Paul's message Luke affirms as in accordance with God's plan and the Scriptures (Acts 28:25–28; Isa. 6:9–10).

Nothing—not a single narrative—falls outside the banner of fulfillment and God's plan. Luke's driving purpose in writing Acts is to show the choppy beginning of the church is still all according to divine plan, his administration.

Overall, the point of Acts is clear. The Father orchestrates all of this according to his will. This is his plan. This is his symphony. This is his masterpiece.

The Word of God

If the plan, purpose, administration of God comes logically first in Acts, then at least one agent of this plan is the *word of God*. Though this theme will be covered more fully in a later chapter, a brief preview is appropriate here.

While we might be tempted to think of the word of God only as the contents of the plan of God, the word has a more active force in Acts and the Bible as a whole. God's agents for his plan are the Son, the Spirit, and his sanctified (his people), but also his word.

In Genesis, God creates by his word. In Isaiah, his word doesn't return to him void (Isa. 55:10–11). In the Gospels and Acts, God's word grows and spreads. In Genesis, Isaiah, and the Gospels, God's plan is to sink his word deep into the soil of the earth so that kingdom trees will multiply.

In Acts, the word appropriately becomes a powerful force through which God conquers.[14] The Spirit empowers the apostles on mission to spread what Luke calls either "the word" or "the word of God/the Lord" (4:31; 8:14, 25; 11:1; 13:5, 7, 44, 46, 48; 16:32; 17:13; 18:11).[15] Luke most commonly describes it as the word *of God*, likely interpreted as a possessive or subjective genitive: God's word. It is the Father's word, his agent.

The word is the Father's agent of new creation and new exodus. It grows and multiplies on the earth, thus becoming a power attributed to God himself. This is most explicitly highlighted in three parallel references in 6:7, 12:24, and 19:20. All of them refer to the word growing, multiplying, and increasing.

These words come directly from the exodus generation who also flourish under persecution (Ex. 1:7, 12, 20). The Father's plan is to establish and grow his community through his word. This is the mission of the triune God.

Table 1.3   The Growth of the Word in Acts

6:7	And the word of God continued to increase, and the number of the disciples multiplied greatly in Jerusalem, and a great many of the priests became obedient to the faith.
12:24	But the word of God increased and multiplied.
19:20	So the word of the Lord continued to increase and prevail mightily.

14 David W. Pao, *Acts and the Isaianic New Exodus* (Eugene, OR: Wipf & Stock, 2016), 150.

15 The "word of God" occurs eleven times in Acts; the "word of the Lord" occurs ten times, and many times "Lord" refers to Jesus, but not exclusively (cf. 8:25; 11:16; 13:44, 48–49; 15:35–36; 16:32; 19:10, 20; 20:35). The "word of his grace" occurs only in 14:3 and 20:32; "word of the gospel" occurs once in 15:7; "word of salvation" in 13:26; and "word" in the absolute sense occurs in the first twenty chapters of Acts.

If the Father is the conductor of this song, then his word is his orchestra. He directs, guides, and spreads his word so that all might hear the kingdom tune.

The Kingdom of God

The plan of God is to spread the word of God. The *content* of this word is the kingdom of God. From a broader biblical perspective, the kingdom message concerns the king's power over the king's people in the king's place.[16] God's plan from the beginning was to exercise his rule over the earth through humans. Humanity failed, so Jesus arrived as the true King who died as their substitute.

When Jesus arrived, he announced the gospel of the kingdom (Luke 4:43). He is the King. He rules over his people and provides a home for them. Acts argues this kingdom plan is still going forward. Two subjects must be addressed here. First, is the kingdom one of Luke's emphases? Second, what is the kingdom message according to Acts?

Admittedly, Luke does not refer to the kingdom of God much in Acts, but he does so at key points, which frames the entire narrative as a continuation of the kingdom story. Two kingdom of God references occur at the beginning of Acts (1:3, 6) and two at the end (28:23, 31), thus bookending the entire narrative. Four references occur in the body of the work at key transition points in the narrative (8:12; 14:22; 19:8; 20:25).

Almost immediately in the narrative of Acts, we see the kingdom is on Luke's mind. The term first appears in Acts 1:3, where it speaks of Jesus teaching his disciples over a period of forty days about the *kingdom of God* before he left. A few verses later, the disciples gather around him and ask, "Lord, will you at this time restore the kingdom to Israel?" (Acts 1:6).

These two references to the kingdom at the beginning of the book create expectations shaping the way we read the rest of the narrative. In

---

16 Patrick Schreiner, *The Kingdom of God and the Glory of the Cross* (Wheaton, IL: Crossway, 2018). Some of the following material is based on my Luke section in that book.

his answer to the disciples, Jesus describes the spread of the kingdom to every place. The Father's plan is for his kingdom to expand.

The double reference to the kingdom reappears at the conclusion of Luke's narrative. In Acts 28:23 and 28:31, Paul is imprisoned in Rome, but Luke's point is the word of God still goes forth. The local Jewish leaders arrange to meet Paul and come to the place where he is staying, and "from morning till evening he expounded to them, testifying to the *kingdom of God*" (Acts 28:23). The last verse of Luke's narrative closes the kingdom framing by speaking of Paul proclaiming the *kingdom of God* "with all boldness and without hindrance" (28:31).

As Alan Thompson explains, in both of "these contexts there is an emphasis on the comprehensive teaching about the kingdom of God."[17] In 1:3, it is Jesus's teaching; 1:6 contains the disciple's question; 28:23 is where Paul is meeting a large number of Jews; and in 28:31, Luke closes his narrative with a summary statement of Paul's preaching. Each of these has a comprehensive summary or conceptual framework summary to the message of both Jesus and Paul.

What many overlook is the kingdom statements in the middle of the narrative. Four key kingdom references occur, mapping onto Luke's geographical progression. After the Jerusalem narrative, readers come across a reference to the kingdom of God in Samaria when Philip preaches the good news about the kingdom of God centered on Jesus Christ and many are baptized (8:12).

Then at the end of Paul's first missionary journey, he travels back through the places he has evangelized and strengthens them, saying that through many tribulations they must enter the kingdom of God (14:22). In Paul's final locale as a free man, Ephesus, he comes into the synagogue and boldly reasons with the people about the kingdom of God (19:8). Finally, in Paul's farewell speech at Miletus, he summarizes his message as "proclaiming the kingdom" (20:25). Each block of Luke's narrative includes at least one reference to the kingdom.

---

17   Alan Thompson, *Acts of the Risen Lord Jesus: Luke's Account of God's Unfolding Plan*, NSBT (Downers Grove, IL: InterVarsity Press, 2011), 44.

Table 1.4   Kingdom of God References in Acts

Acts 1–7 (Galilee/Jerusalem)	Acts 1:3, 6
Acts 8–12 (Judea and Samaria)	Acts 8:12
Acts 13–20 (Paul's Journeys)	Acts 14:22; 19:8; 20:25
Acts 21–28 (Paul's Trials)	Acts 28:23, 31

However, this raises the question: If the apostles proclaim the kingdom, then where is it? Luke's answer to this comes in Acts 1:6–8 when the disciples ask if Jesus is going to restore the kingdom at this time? Jesus answers with a "no, not now" in 1:7 and then "yes, now" in 1:8. To put this another way, Jesus seems to give a "Not Yet" and "Already" answer in 1:7–8.

In 1:7, Jesus says no: "It is not for you to know times or seasons that the Father has fixed by his own authority." The consummation of the kingdom plan is set by the Father. So he rejects their attempt to calculate the timing. However, he goes on to say yes in 1:8: "But you will receive power when the Holy Spirit has come upon you, and you will be my witnesses in Jerusalem, and in all Judea and Samaria, and to the end of the earth."

Therefore, when the disciples ask if he is going to restore the kingdom to Israel, he reframes how they are to think of it in terms of receiving the Holy Spirit and welcoming more into the kingdom life.

This transitions us to the second issue: the content of the kingdom message in Acts. Luke, as a specific author of scripture, emphasizes particular aspects of the kingdom. He focuses both on *Jesus as the Savior and King, and the upside-down nature of the kingdom—more specifically, the people welcomed into the kingdom.*

If the kingdom is the message of the apostles, then at the center of this message is Jesus. Without Jesus, there is no kingdom. He is the King, the inaugurator, the ruler, and the Suffering Servant of the kingdom. His life, death, resurrection, and ascension are the key to understanding the kingdom. Without him, the kingdom plan is dead in its tracks.

All of Jesus's actions are oriented toward the goal of welcoming more into the kingdom. He dies for his people, he lives so that they too might have life, and he ascends so they too might be glorified. Luke specifically puts emphasis on the "surprising" converts to the kingdom. Jesus does this in Luke as he proclaims good news to the poor, liberty to the captives, recovery of sight to the blind, liberty for those who are oppressed, and the year of the Lord's favor (Luke 4:18–19). Jesus says the Spirit of the Lord anoints him to do these things.

Then in Acts, this same Spirit anoints his followers as they go out and welcome the marginal into this kingdom plan. Luke's picture of the people of the kingdom was culturally and ethically daring. They welcome the marginal, the rejected, the poor, tax collectors, sinners, women, Samaritans, and Gentiles. It is the lame, the eunuch, the Samaritans, those of backwater towns, and barbarians who respond to the good news of the kingdom.

This radical kingdom message drove the religious leaders to seek the apostles' execution. The symbolic universe Jesus created challenged the status quo and angered those around him. God's plan was to create a new kingdom community where the oppressed and poor were welcome.

The Spirit initiates hospitality toward these groups through miracles, rescues God's people, and judges God's enemies. Miracles abound in Acts. The lame are healed (3:1–10; 14:8–10), buildings are shaken (4:31), apostles are set free by the angel of the Lord (5:17–21), Philip is transported by the Spirit (8:40), light appears to Saul (9:1–9), Saul is blinded and healed (9:8–19), Aeneas is healed (9:32–35), Dorcas is restored to life (9:36–41), Herod is struck down (12:20–23), Elymas is blinded (13:6–11), demons are cast out (16:16–18), Paul is freed by an earthquake (16:25–27), Eutychus is raised from the dead (20:7–12), Paul is unaffected by a snake bite (28:3–5), and the father of Publius is healed (28:8).

If the apostles and other Christians needed certainty concerning God's plan, then the miracles give evidence that God's kingdom plan is happening in the present. The kingdom is present by the Spirit. The miracles point to the presence of Jesus's kingdom in the midst of

Satan's. Luke interprets those who are lame, imprisoned, and blinded as "oppressed by the devil" (10:38) and the role of the apostles is to turn people from darkness to light, or from the power of Satan to God (26:18). A cosmic and apocalyptic battle unfolds on the pages of Acts. To domesticate it does violence to a plain reading of the text.

Conclusion

I began this chapter with a conductor who orchestrates a symphony. The Father is the conductor of all things. Luke doesn't depart from good Jewish theology. A prewritten and beautiful end to God's story is coming, and Acts fits into this drama.

A theology of Acts thus logically begins with the one who orchestrates, with the plan of God, the word of God, the kingdom of God. All of Acts thus fulfills God's plans. Acts is a fulfillment document.

Every human being is tempted to think the story of the universe centers on them, but Acts reminds us this is primarily God's story and we are simply included in it. We can either play a part in furthering his purpose or oppose it. If we oppose it, we will be crushed and crush ourselves along the way. If we step into God's administration, there may be persecution and pain, but there will also be great contentment.

Later, we will look to more participants in the Father's symphony, but here we focused on the word of God. The word is personified in Acts; it is a divine agent. It conquers in the midst of opposition; it grows and multiplies. The Father's plan is executed through the word.

The content of this word is the kingdom of God. It is his plan for the earth. A new King has stepped onto the scene and is remaking all things, starting with this little community. God's administration is good. Through his King, he is welcoming all to his side. This includes the poor, the ethnically other, women, and the socially ostracized.

All of the other themes in Acts, and their subsidiary themes, are in some way linked to God the Father and his plan. The Father has decisively interrupted history through the sending of the Son and the Spirit, and not seeing the Father's role in all of Luke's recounting overlooks a major refrain, if not the major refrain.

Christ Lives and Rules

Let all the house of Israel therefore know for
certain that God has made him both Lord and
Christ, this Jesus whom you crucified.

ACTS 2:36

Lift Up Your Eyes

I enjoy going to concerts, but in this stage of my life, it happens infrequently. However, while in Oregon, my wife and I began to get to know the members of Beautiful Eulogy, a hip-hop group based in Portland. One night, we decided to go and see them live at a venue downtown called The Doug Fir Lounge.

Hearing a group at home is one thing. Hearing them live is another. At a live show, you feel the music. The bass vibrates your chest. It makes your heart beat a few paces faster. In the Beautiful Eulogy album *Worthy*, they sing of Jesus's sovereignty. Thomas Terry in their spoken-word "Immanuel" proclaims the following lines:

Lift up your eyes and see the riches of the
All-sufficient King seated on his throne in glory
See his scepter that stretches the expanse of unmeasured space

Hear Him who holds all things together declare
"All things are mine without exception"

In many ways, this is the message of Acts. Readers must lift up their eyes to see the King. He resides in heaven now. No longer is he present physically, but his scepter stretches over all space based on his resurrection and ascension.

All things are his, so he sends his disciples into all nations. Acts is about the Father's plan, but the Father's plan centralizes, coheres, and climaxes in the Son. For it is the Son who lives, rules, and directs—even while bodily absent.

Many works on Acts begin with a popular but mistaken focus on the apostles or the Holy Spirit. Luke begins in a different way: with his eyes fixed on Jesus. The first verse sets up Acts not so much as a work of the apostles, or merely the work of the Holy Spirit, but the continued work of the risen and enthroned Jesus (1:1–2).[1]

Luke tells Theophilus about what Jesus "began" to do and teach in his first volume (Acts 1:1). The word "began" refers to someone initiating an action, but not completing it. Jesus continues his work in Luke's second volume. His life and rule are ongoing, even in his exalted state. The new era has arrived; the revolution continues.

Luke is the only author to offer an actual account of Jesus's departure. In fact, he does so twice, once at the end of his Gospel (Luke 24:50–53) and once at the beginning of Acts (1:9–11). Some have argued that because of this, Acts exhibits an "absentee Christology." While it is true Jesus is physically absent in most of Acts, the focus is not so much on his absence or inactivity "but rather *the place* from which Jesus rules for the rest of Acts."[2]

The resurrection and ascension (exaltation) becomes the hinge on which Luke's two-volume work turns, a watershed event determining and directing the rest of the narrative. Luke affirms the resurrection-

---

1   Alan Thompson, *The Acts of the Risen Lord Jesus: Luke's Account of God's Unfolding Plan*, NSBT (Downers Grove, IL: InterVarsity Press, 2011), 48.

2   Thompson, *The Acts of the Risen Lord Jesus*, 49; emphasis added.

ascension proves Jesus is the Messiah and Lord.[3] This explains why Jesus is called Lord more in Acts than in Luke.

If the Father's plan is to plant his word, then this word centers on the living and exalted King. The only way humans can have peace with one another, and the good news go to the nations, is through a new righteous King of Israel. Therefore, at the center of the kingdom message is a royal throne. As Jay-Z and Kayne West said, watch the throne.[4]

Essentially, Luke lays out his theological précis in Acts 1–2 and Peter's sermon interprets it. The plan of God was to send the Spirit, yet the Spirit's arrival was predicated on the death, rising, and exaltation of Jesus. The Son therefore *precedes* the Spirit, and the Spirit *proceeds* from the Father and Son.

Jesus is declared "Lord and Christ" because of his victory (2:36). His universal lordship means universal mission. While Peter connects Jesus's resurrection and ascension, he also distinguishes between them. Therefore, I will do the same as they speak to different realities.

This chapter will examine Jesus's life and rule as central themes for Luke's second volume. I will begin with his resurrection (life), then move to his ascension (rule), and then finally argue for the significance of the cross (death) in Acts.

Table 2.1   Jesus's Death, Life, and Rule

The Resurrection	Jesus *lives* forever as the Davidic King, providing the hope of life.
The Ascension	Jesus *reigns* forever, providing direction for his people.
The Cross	Jesus *submits* to death, providing forgiveness of sins.

3 Bock argues that Luke's two volumes move from identifying Jesus as Messiah-Servant-Prophet to seeing him as Lord. While I think there is some truth to this, 2:36 and the sermons in Acts prove both his messianic identity and lordship. Darrell L. Bock, *A Theology of Luke and Acts: God's Promised Program, Realized for All Nations*, ed. Andreas J. Köstenberger (Grand Rapids, MI: Zondervan, 2012), 177–84.

4 Jay-Z and Kanye West, *Watch the Throne* (Manhattan: Def Jam, Roc Nation, Roc-A-Fella, 2011).

Jesus's Resurrection

Though the resurrection is not recounted in Acts, Jesus's new life is a major artery in Luke's work, giving vivacity to his body and the world.[5] The Father's plan is to give life to the world through Jesus.

The first character on the scene is the resurrected Jesus. Jesus "presented himself alive to them [the disciples] after his suffering by many proofs" (1:3). Then after the apostles' commission (1:8), Peter explicitly notes they are resurrection witnesses (1:22).

One of our earliest interpreters, John Chrysostom, thus calls Acts "a demonstration of the resurrection."[6] Daniel Marguerat likewise says the resurrection is the heart of the message of Luke-Acts.[7] Resurrection *speeches* and resurrection *signs* dot the landscape of Acts. The new era with the offer of life has commenced.

Resurrection Speeches

The resurrection is central in the *speeches* of Acts. They could even be labeled as resurrection reports. Jesus's messengers go about preaching the presence of new life. This is true for Peter, Paul, and the other messengers in Acts.

In Peter's Pentecost speech, he explains the presence of the Spirit by pointing to Jesus's resurrection. After quoting from Joel 2, Luke allocates eleven verses to the divine necessity of Jesus's resurrection (Acts 2:22–32). The falling of the Spirit is built upon Jesus's resurrection (Acts 2:24; cf. Ps. 16:8–11). The new era is here because Jesus conquered the tomb.

Peter's second sermon explains Jesus raised the lame man. The message has a clear resurrection *inclusio* (Acts 3:13, 26) and several details

---

5 This language of artery comes from Brandon D. Crowe, *The Hope of Israel: The Resurrection of Christ in the Acts of the Apostles* (Grand Rapids, MI: Baker Academic, 2020), 5.

6 Chrysostom, Homily 1 on Acts, in *NPNF*, Series 1, vol. 11, ed. Philip Schaff (Grand Rapids, MI: Eerdmans, 1925), 3.

7 Daniel Marguerat, "Luc-Actes: La Résurrection à l'oeuvre Dans l'historie," in *Résurrection: L'après-Mort Dans Le Monde Ancient et Le Nouveau Testament*, ed. Odette Mainville and Daniel Marguerat (Geneva: Labor et Fides, 2001), 195–214, cited in Crowe, *The Hope of Israel*, x, 6; and Kevin L. Anderson, *But God Raised Him from the Dead: The Theology of Jesus's Resurrection in Luke-Acts* (Eugene, OR: Wipf & Stock, 2007).

point to resurrection tropes. Peter marks Jesus with multiple titles. He is the Holy and Righteous One (3:14) and the Author, Champion, or Pioneer of Life (3:15). These speak to Christ's abundant life.

He was innocent as the Holy and Righteous One, so God reversed the sentence of death. And Jesus is now the Author of Life because of his defeat of death. Therefore, the people shouldn't be amazed at the lame man walking. Resurrection life marks the new era (3:12).

Peter's third sermon uses the good deed they did in the healing of the lame man (4:9) to springboard immediately to Jesus's resurrection: it is through this raised one that the man is raised (4:10). After Peter and John are thrown into prison, the angel of the Lord releases them with the instructions to return to the temple and speak to the people "all the words of this Life" (5:20). When they are castigated, they say they must preach that "the God of our fathers raised Jesus, whom you killed" (5:30).

Though Stephen's speech does not reference the resurrection, the entire point is the expansive presence of God in Jesus. If the temple was where people met God, now they meet God in Jesus who is alive. Stephen's speech climaxes in a heavenly vision of the resurrected Lord as he dies.

The final major speech from Peter is to Cornelius in Acts 10:34–48. Though it might not seem like the resurrection would prove central to Gentiles, it does in two ways. First, Peter affirms Jesus is the Christ, the Lord of all (10:36). In the context of speaking to a centurion in Caesarea (named after Caesar), this is a clear antithetical claim to Caesar's lordship. Second, Jesus's lordship is supported by the fact that Jesus lived, died, and was raised from the dead (10:40). He is the forever king unlike Caesar. The apostles are witnesses to this. Jesus is the judge of the living and the dead (10:42).

Paul's speeches likewise center on the resurrection and the life that comes through Jesus. All his preaching is birthed from his vision of the resurrected Jesus in Acts 9. In Pisidian Antioch (13:16–41), Paul focuses on Jesus as Savior and the provider of salvation but, like Peter, speaks of Jesus's execution and God's reversal of that verdict (13:30,

33–37). The whole speech leads to light going to the Gentiles. "The Gentile mission is under way *because of* Jesus's resurrection."[8]

This is further evidenced by James's speech at the Council when he says God will rebuild the tent of David, quoting from Amos 9 (Acts 15:16). This language of building echoes 2 Samuel 7:13 and the building of David's house and *raising up* his throne forever. David's forever throne can be established only by one who lives forever.

The Gentile mission and the resurrection are intertwined again in Paul's famous sermon to philosophers at Athens. Some Epicureans and Stoics label him an amateur philosopher because he preaches Jesus and the resurrection (Acts 17:18).[9] The idea of the dead rising was a novel one to the Greeks and therefore this was a new teaching to their ears. For the rest of the sermon, Paul gives Adam and creation theology, but he returns to the resurrection, saying God will judge the world. The one raised from the dead is appointed to be the judge (17:31).

In Paul's trials, the resurrection is again dominant. Before the Sanhedrin, Paul claims he is accused because of his hope in the resurrection of the dead (23:6). Though one might be tempted to think Paul merely saw an avenue to play party politics, the larger narrative proves one should not think of this merely as a clever ploy. Paul again brings up the resurrection in the trials with Felix (24:15, 20–21), Festus (25:19), Agrippa (26:6–8, 23), and the Jews in Rome (28:20). Paul's message concerns the hope of the resurrection. He aptly turns his death trials into a resurrection testimony.

Paul summarizes his message as "hope" or the "hope of Israel" (28:20). The terminology for "hope" is used seven time in Acts to refer to resurrection. Paul has hope and preaches hope because Jesus's resurrection is the firstfruits. Many more will follow.

---

8   Crowe, *The Hope of Israel*, 65.

9   The Greek language is unique here and could be translated as "Jesus and *Anastasia*" implying they heard him proclaiming a divine pair, both male and female (foreign deities). Zeus had Themis (Order), Athena carried Nike (Victory), Aphrodite was accompanied by Love, and Jesus had *Anastasia*.

In summary, the messages in Acts are resurrection reports. The theme of Jesus's new life runs a straight and consistent thread through Acts because it is a central part of God's plan. The message of Acts is resurrection life is here!

Resurrection Signs

The resurrection continues not only in the speeches but through narrative *signs* as people are healed and rescued. Though most are prone to see the resurrection in the speeches, Jesus's life is more expansive and extensive. Resurrection is not only preached but also enacted; not only proclaimed but also personified.

For example, when Peter and John first go into the temple, they take the temple beggar by the right hand and raise him up (3:7). The resurrection trope is clear by the term "raised him up" (*ēgeiren*), which is the word used most commonly for resurrection. Then, Peter defends this act when they are questioned by pointing to Jesus's resurrection life (4:10).

Resurrection signs occur again when the apostles escape from prison. The Sanhedrin imprisons them overnight (5:18–19), but the angel of the Lord opens the prison doors, mirroring the angel rolling away the stone at Christ's grave.

Stephen's stoning provides another example. Though Luke does not report the resurrection of Stephen, it is clearly anticipated by the parallels with Jesus's trial and death. Both Jesus and Stephen are brought before their own leaders (Luke 22:66; Acts 6:9); false witnesses rise up (Luke 23:2; Acts 6:11–13); priests question them (Luke 22:66–67; Acts 7:1); Jesus and Stephen speak of the Son of Man (Luke 22:69; Acts 7:55–56); their testimony incites violence (Luke 22:71; Acts 7:54, 57–59); they commit their spirits to God (Luke 23:46; Acts 7:59); they ask God to forgive their opponents (Luke 23:34; Acts 7:60). Jesus rises from the dead; Stephen sees the Son of Man standing at the right hand of God (Acts 7:55–56).

Philip performs signs, including the healing of the paralyzed and lame in Samaria (8:7). Saul is blinded for three days, unable to eat or drink (9:8–9) and then receives his sight, is baptized, and takes food

(9:12, 18–19). Saul's reception of the Spirit and baptism are symbolic for his resurrection (Rom. 6:3–11). Peter raises Aeneas from his bed (Acts 9:34) and commands Tabitha to arise (9:40). Both of these are tremors of resurrection upheaval.

Paul, like Peter, raises a lame man, telling him to stand up and walk (14:8–10). Then Paul himself experiences a resurrection of sorts at Lystra when he is stoned by the Jews from Antioch and Iconium and is presumed dead. However, Luke calmly says "he rose up and entered the city" (14:19–20). Eutychus also experiences a resurrection. He sinks into a deep sleep (20:9), a metaphor in the Scriptures for death, falls into the darkness, and is presumed dead. But Paul goes into the darkness, takes him in his arms, brings him back into the house with light, and gives him food (20:10–11).

On the sea journey to Rome, Paul both experiences resurrection and spreads resurrection life. Paul prophesies, provides food, becomes the source of salvation for those on the boat, and receives visions of encouragement along his way.

On Malta, a venomous snake bites Paul, but he shakes it off (28:3–6).[10] Paul is saved through the water and then he is bitten by a snake. This narrative pattern mirrors not only Eden but also the exodus generation, and Jesus as well. Each figure travels through water and then encounters snakes. Brandon Crowe even notes the message could be that the sting of the serpent's bite is rendered impotent by Christ's work (1 Cor. 15:55–56).[11]

The point of all this is the Father's plan in Acts is to spread resurrection life through the gift of his Son. The apostles not only *witness* to the resurrection; they also *perform* resurrection. Any reading of Acts that neglects the resurrection neglects the heart of the message offered to all.

Jesus's Ascension

Though often neglected, Jesus's ascension also needs to be included in a theology of Acts. Luke's favorite honorific for Jesus is "Lord," and this

---

10 Like Taylor Swift.

11 Crowe, *The Hope of Israel*, 84.

is based on his exaltation. Though the title "Son of Man" occurs only once (Acts 7:56), the Danielic background is the basis for much of the theology of Acts. Daniel syndicates Jesus's universal sovereignty with the nation's submission:

"I saw in the night visions,

> and behold, with the clouds of heaven
>> there came one like a son of man,
> and he came to the Ancient of Days
>> and was presented before him.
> And to him was given dominion
>> and glory and a kingdom,
> that all peoples, nations, and languages
>> should serve him;
> his dominion is an everlasting dominion,
>> which shall not pass away,
> and his kingdom one
>> that shall not be destroyed. (Dan. 7:13–14)

In the same way, Acts indicates Jesus's exaltation means the nations are now called to submit to this new King. Jesus's ascension is thus no afterthought or meaningless rubber stamp upon the resurrection.[12] It is an event in its own right.

The resurrection and ascension should be related, but they should not be equated. As Murray Harris explained, "The resurrection proclaims, 'He lives—and that forever'; the Exaltation proclaims, 'He reigns—and that forever.'"[13] In most of the speeches in Acts, the narrative of the Bible, and the early creeds of the church, the ascension is recounted as a separate event from the resurrection.

---

12 Patrick Schreiner, *The Ascension of Christ: Recovering a Neglected Doctrine* (Bellingham, WA: Lexham, 2020).

13 Murray Harris, *Raised Immortal: Resurrection and Immortality in the New Testament* (Grand Rapids, MI: Eerdmans, 1983), 85.

For example, in the programmatic Pentecost sermon, Peter argues the Spirit has come because Jesus has been exalted. He first speaks of Jesus's resurrection with scriptural support (Acts 2:22–32; cf. Ps. 16:8–11), *and then* of Jesus's ascension with scriptural support (Acts 2:33–36; cf. Ps. 110:1). Both of these events install Jesus as Lord and Messiah (Acts 2:36), but they are distinct events.

Parsons argues the ascension sets into motion the entire book of Acts.[14] The ascension occurs at the beginning of Acts and narratively spurs on the rest of the action. Jesus can only spread life because he has been exalted to the heavens and the Spirit has come. Jesus's ascension marks not the cessation of his work, but the continuation and even exaltation of his Messianic vocation.

Acts therefore is based on the fundamental reality of the continuing reign of the living *and* enthroned Christ. Other themes in Acts spring forth and grow out of Christ's enthronement. As one scholar has put it, "the ascension is for Luke the point of intersection of Christology, eschatology, and ecclesiology."[15] Without reigning as Lord in heaven, Christ's work is incomplete. The ascension is central to a theology of Acts for a whole host of reasons.

First, Jesus's ascension forms Luke's geographical imagination. If geography is central to the structure of Acts, then *the place* where the risen Jesus reigns is the theological root for narrative fruit. He now continues to direct the affairs of the church from heaven.

Heaven is the space and sphere from which all reality is ruled and judged. From the heavenly throne, salvation proceeds into time and space. The spread of the gospel *geographically* is inseparable from Christ's cosmic reign in the heavens. Earthly space is reordered by the heavenly Christ.

Second, Jesus's ascension enthrones him as the one with supreme authority, painting the book under the hues of spiritual warfare. Though

---

14 Mikeal C. Parsons, *The Departure of Jesus in Luke-Acts: The Ascension Narratives in Context*, LNTS (Sheffield: JSOT Press, 1987).

15 See the note in Douglas Farrow, *Ascension and Ecclesia: On the Significance of the Doctrine of the Ascension for Ecclesiology and Christian Cosmology* (Grand Rapids, MI: Eerdmans, 1999), 16n6.

Satan is not mentioned much in Acts (5:3; 10:38; 13:10; 26:18), the concept is ever present from the beginning as it is the Spirit who works.

As Justus Jonas said, "When [Jesus] ascended he took captive captivity, that is, sin, death, hell and the kingdom of the devil."[16] And when Jesus ascended, he gave gifts (apostles, prophets, evangelists, shepherds, and teachers) to his church (Eph. 4:11). In Luke's Gospel, Jesus arrived announcing he came to release captives (Luke 4:18). This is interpreted in the narrative as those ensnared by the devil (Acts 10:38).

Therefore, Jesus's ascension confirms the continuation of the upside-down kingdom. He overturns privilege, ethnic superiority, and gender hierarchy. He challenges Caesar's *Pax Romana* and welcomes the least of these. Rome is animated by the forces of darkness, which are conquered in Christ's exaltation where he is enthroned above all powers and authorities.

Third, much of the theology of Acts stems from Christ's exalted status. Peter's Pentecost sermon places a major emphasis on Jesus's resurrection and ascension. Throughout Acts, the apostles and Luke himself refer to Jesus as Lord (1:21; 4:33; 5:14, 40–41; 8:16; 9:3–6, 10–16, 35, 42; 10:13–15; 14:3; 16:14; 18:9–10; 22:17–21; 23:11). Acts exists because Jesus is Lord. The church exists because Jesus is Lord.

The sending of the Spirit also stems from Jesus's ascension. Peter explains in his Pentecost sermon that Jesus's ascension and the pouring out of the Spirit are linked: "Being therefore exalted at the right hand of God . . . he has poured out this that you yourselves are seeing and hearing" (Acts 2:33). Jesus's body pierces the barrier between heaven and earth in his ascension. It is the ascended Lord who *sends the Holy Spirit* to his people. Jesus is the baptizer—the Anointed anointer (John 1:33).

Christ's ascension deserves better narrative positioning in our reading of Acts. It is the backbone of the geographical story. It is where Christ's authority over the devil is affirmed. It is vital to the sending of the Spirit. Without the ascension, the story of Christ's work in Acts is

---

16 Annotations on Acts 1:9. Esther Chung-Kim and Todd R. Hains, eds., *Acts: New Testament*, vol. 6, Reformation Commentary on Scripture (Downers Grove, IL: IVP Academic, 2014), 10.

incomplete. Without it, our good news is truncated. Without it, Christ is not declared Lord and Messiah. The Son of God did not come down to earth to stay. He came down in order that he might ascend—and one day descend again.

Jesus's Continued Ministry in Acts

Jesus's ascension not only authorizes and endorses Jesus's work but also *continues* Christ's work. Though Jesus left the earthly stage, he never left the biblical stage. He labored on the earth; now he labors in heaven. As Peter Orr states, "Christians have tended to focus their attention on what Jesus has done (his life, death and resurrection) and what he will do (return and reign)."[17] Studies on what Christ is doing now or what happened after the resurrection are relatively rare.

The enthroned Jesus appears at key moments in Acts, showing he is still active. Jesus reveals himself to Stephen (Acts 7:55–56), Saul (9:5; 22:8–10; 26:14–18), Ananias (9:10–15), Cornelius (10:4), Peter (10:12–16), and Paul on multiple occasions (18:9–11; 22:17–21; 23:11). This is not even including the work of the Spirit—who is called the Spirit of Jesus (16:7) and Spirit of the Lord (5:9; 8:39)—or the angel of the Lord (5:19; 8:26; 12:7, 11, 17, 23). As Leslie Houlden said, in Acts Jesus has an "obstinate presence."[18]

And as Jesus was the prophet, priest, and king on the earth, so he is our prophet, priest, and king in heaven. These perpetual offices are vital for any reading of Acts. Though some might think Luke doesn't give much thought to Jesus as prophet, priest, or king, this is simply not true. A community who proclaims Christ continues the prophetic strain. The temple theme in Acts necessarily includes priesthood themes. And kingship realities are ever present as they call people to pledge loyalty to Jesus.

Jesus was a prophet on earth. He proclaimed God's word, performed signs and wonders, and was empowered by the Spirit. These actions

---

17 Peter C. Orr, *Exalted Above the Heavens: The Risen and Ascended Christ*, NSBT 47 (Downers Grove, IL: IVP Academic, 2019), 1.

18 J. L. Houlden, "Beyond Belief: Preaching the Ascension, II," *Theology* 94 (May/June 1991): 174.

didn't cease upon his ascent. His prophetic work continues. In fact, he multiplies and democratizes his prophetic work by the Spirit whom he poured out on the apostles. The church now proclaims Jesus as his prophetic mouthpiece (Acts 2:11). His people perform signs and wonders in his name and they receive the same empowering Spirit. This theme is ever present in Acts as the apostles heal in Jesus's name and preach in Jesus's name. They continue Christ's prophetic work.

Jesus's ascension also marks a turn in his priestly role. Jesus was a priest on the earth, but now he is a priest in heaven. Not many see priestly themes in Acts, so I will spend more time here. Luke emphasizes Jesus's priestly role in both of his ascension accounts. First, Luke points to Jesus's priestly blessing as he is carried up into heaven at the end of his Gospel:

> And he led them out as far as Bethany, and lifting up his hands he blessed them. While he blessed them, he parted from them and was carried up into heaven. (Luke 24:50–51)

Though priests served before God, they brought these blessings to God's people. In the Old Testament, as the high priest left the tent of meeting, he would lift up his hands and bless the people (Lev. 9:22–23). This was modeled after both Moses and Melchizedek who blessed Israel and Abraham. Numbers provides the content of the priestly blessing:

> The LORD bless you and keep you;
> the LORD make his face to shine upon you and be gracious to you;
> the LORD lift up his countenance upon you and give you peace.
>   (Num. 6:24–26)

Luke's point is that Jesus blesses us in a similar way as our high priest. Jesus is the new Aaron who extends his hands over the people and gives them peace through the Holy Spirit. His priestly blessing gifts the Spirit—the one who allows peace. Jesus not only gives the Aaronic blessing; he fulfills it.

Second, Luke redoubles on the priestly themes in the recount of Jesus's ascension in Acts 1:9–11, with the reference to the clouds, angels, and Jesus's rising:

> And when he had said these things, as they were looking on, he was lifted up, and a cloud took him out of their sight. And while they were gazing into heaven as he went, behold, two men stood by them in white robes, and said, "Men of Galilee, why do you stand looking into heaven? This Jesus, who was taken up from you into heaven, will come in the same way as you saw him go into heaven."

If you think back to the Old Testament, a priest would "go up" into the temple or tabernacle. This action was based on Moses's ascent of Mount Sinai, where fire and smoke filled the mountain (Ex. 13:21; 19:9; 24:15; 34:5; 40:38). Now those of Aaron's descent go into the presence of God. And when they go into God's presence, there is smoke (Lev. 16:2; Num. 12:5; Isa. 19:1; Ezek. 1:4; 10:4). Not only that but the two men, likely angels, signify that Jesus has gone into the Holy of Holies.

The priestly theme continues as the Spirit comes at Pentecost and the narrative continually returns to the temple location and theme as well as the theme of prayer (Acts 1:14; 1:24; 2:42; 4:31; 6:4, 6; 8:15; 9:11, 40; 10:2, 9, 30–31; 11:5; 12:5, 12; 13:3 14:23; 16:25; 20:36; 21:5; 28:8). The church can press on in the midst of persecution only because she calls out to the one who intercedes for her in heaven.

Finally, and most importantly, Christ's ascension marks a turn in his kingly vocation. Christ's kingship is not complete until he rises and goes before the Father in heaven (1:9–11). He now rules over all in a unique way after his return to the Father.

Jesus did not get taken by a cloud to go rest in heaven because his work was finished. Sitting implies he is free from all disturbance and opposition. His bodily work on the earth was complete for a time, but now he rules from heaven—where God resides. He directs the affairs of the world from this exalted position. But the ascension also affirms the church is a waiting people (1:11). They await his return and the consummation of his rule upon the earth (Ps. 110:1).

Christ's rule doesn't mean the church is called to go out and rule the world. Nor does the kingship of Christ immediately eliminate the harsh and wretched conditions of life for Christ's legion. Christ's kingship is in heaven, and therefore the church's royalty is hidden, for now, with him.

The ascension of Christ is thus critical for any reading of Acts because if the resurrection proclaims the *life* of Jesus continues, then the ascension declares the *rule* of Jesus forever.

The Messiah's ascension provides the foundation for the geographical mission, the sending of the Spirit, the conquering of the devil, and his continued work as prophet, priest, and king. The apostles witness to Jesus's exaltation. Any reading of Acts that neglects the Christological culmination of this work will be skewed from the start.

Jesus's Death in Acts

Some have questioned, others have denied, an emphasis on the cross in Luke. Do the cross, atonement, and sacrificial aspects of Christ's work function as centrally in Luke's writing as in other New Testament authors?

Good work has been done showing its presence in his Gospel. The question remains as to what role Christ's sacrifice plays in Acts. Though the emphasis does lie on the exaltation of Christ, this does not mean the cross is absent or unimportant. Rather, the humiliation and exaltation should be viewed in unison.

First, the cross-resurrection-ascension are all a single script in the minds the New Testament authors, as well as in the two-volume Luke-Acts. Luke's Gospel spends a significant amount of time on the cross, which must inform Acts. The resurrection-ascension confirms and validates the victory on the cross. This is seen in Acts 3–4, as Jesus is labelled the "servant" who gives life (3:13, 26; 4:25, 27, 30). Without the cross, neither resurrection nor ascension happens or has significance attached to it. Alternatively, without the resurrection-ascension, the cross is merely a tragic miscarriage of justice against a first-century

Jewish rabbi. The resurrection and the ascent validate what happened on the cross.

Second, David Moffitt has argued that Luke connects forgiveness and purification with Jesus's exaltation.[19] The ascension is the culminating sacrificial act as Jesus conveys the materials of the sacrifice into God's presence and presents his blood by approaching the true altar in heaven. Acts notably begins with Jesus's ascent, thus putting the whole book under the banner of blood, forgiveness, and purification.

Third, the Spirit arrives as the Spirit of Christ, who applies his work of redemption. The Spirit applies blood and washes by water. Without the Spirit's application of redemption, no salvation ensues. Without Christ's atoning death, the Spirit has no redemption to apply. All four Gospels proclaim the outpouring of the Spirit is the work of Christ who has accomplished redemption. Jesus gives them the Spirit, and the Spirit gives them Jesus.

Fourth, Luke showcases the cross through the life of his followers, the servants.[20] Luke's portrait of Jesus's death is more indirect, allusive, and embodied than explicit in Acts. Jesus is the suffering servant and the apostles are the Servant's servants. Luke's narrative highlights Jesus's journey to Jerusalem, which is his journey to his death. The apostles likewise will suffer in Jerusalem, and then Paul will travel to Jerusalem and Rome in order to be on trial like Jesus. In Luke, Jesus is presented as the innocent and righteous sufferer. This theme receives due attention in Acts as the apostles are presented as righteous sufferers who carry the aroma of Jesus's death (3:13, 18, 26; 4:27; 7:57–60; 8:32–33; 23–26).

Fifth, the apostles consistently preach the forgiveness of sins and salvation, which are explicitly tied to Jesus's death (2:38; 3:19; 5:31; 8:22; 10:43; 13:38; 26:18). Luke continually emphasizes that Jesus's death is according to the plan and will of God (1:16; 2:23; 3:18; 4:28; 13:27, 29;

---

19 David M. Moffitt, "Atonement at the Right Hand: The Sacrificial Significance of Jesus' Exaltation in Acts," *NTS* 62, no. 4 (2016): 549–68.

20 Beers argues the extension of the servant theme to the disciples might partly explain the supposed silence of atonement theology. Holly Beers, *The Followers of Jesus as the "Servant": Luke's Model from Isaiah for the Disciples in Luke-Acts* (London: Bloomsbury T&T Clark, 2016), 177.

17:3). When Paul says farewell to the Ephesian elders, he mentions that God has obtained the church with his own blood (20:28). When the apostles break bread, they reenact the covenant meal, which focused on the body and blood of Jesus (2:42, 46; 20:7; 27:35).

Therefore, the cross is not absent in Acts. The second volume emphasizes Jesus's exalted state, but this is always connected to Christ's atonement. In addition, the cross comes into play to a great extent in the lives of his followers as they are persecuted and die like their Savior.

Excursus: Christology in Acts

Jesus is the one who continues to work in Acts, yet we also must look to how Luke characterizes Jesus. The sermons in Acts give a retrospective view on Jesus, and much of Luke's theology of Jesus can be found in the titles he bestows upon Jesus. Luke most frequently characterizes Jesus as Lord and Messiah. Yet he also labels him humble servant, Savior, Son of God, Son of Man, and the Holy and Innocent One.

Most foundationally for Luke, Jesus is Lord and Messiah.[a] Jesus is the anointed and exalted King, the embodiment of Yahweh himself (10:36). Peter's climactic conclusion to his Pentecost speech sets the stage for the narrative as a whole. Because of Jesus's life and victory, Peter states,

Let all the house of Israel therefore know for certain that God has made him both Lord and Christ, this Jesus whom you crucified. (2:36)

Though it might seem like this has adoptionistic hues with the language of "made," this is not the case. This is not adoptionistic Christology but rather the story of how Jesus was *appointed* from long ago (even before time began), *designated* in his life and baptism, and then *enthroned* as God-man Lord and Messiah at his ascension.

Luke has labeled Jesus as Lord before he ascends to the heavens (1:6). He is Lord in the womb of Mary (Luke 1:43); John the Baptist goes before the Lord (Luke 1:76; 3:4), which clearly refers to Jesus; the angels declare Jesus is Lord (Luke 2:11); the Spirit of the Lord is upon Jesus (Luke 4:18); and Peter and the man with leprosy confess Jesus is Lord (Luke 5:8, 12). In Acts, Jesus is addressed as Lord before he ascends to the Father (Acts 1:6).

However, Luke also recognizes Jesus *will be* great and *will be* called the Son of the Most High (Luke 1:32). As Ben Witherington explains, "It was not that Jesus became *someone* different from who he was before, but that he entered a new stage in his career, or assumed new roles after the ascension."[b]

Rowe says the making of which Acts 2:36 speaks is not ontological transformation but an epistemological shift in the perception of the human community.[c] However, it is not only an epistemological shift but also an epochal shift because Jesus is installed in honor at God's right hand. To put this another way, the Lord was made Lord. He was Lord of the universe before his birth and now he is the *messianic Lord* who has accomplished God's will as a man but never emptied himself of his divinity while on the earth.

Luke also presents Jesus as the suffering servant who humbled himself but was raised up (Isa. 52:13–53:12). He is Lord and Messiah *because* he was the wise king who humbled himself even to the point of death. "Behold, my servant shall act wisely; he shall be high and lifted up, and shall be exalted" (Isa. 52:13). Peter speaks of Jesus as the glorified servant (Acts

3:13), the raised servant (3:26), the anointed servant (4:27), the holy servant (4:30), and the cut and humble servant (8:32–33).

The Philip and Eunuch narrative in Acts 8:32–33 pairs the servant's humiliation and exaltation, quoting from Isaiah 53:7–8:

> Like a sheep he was led to the slaughter
>> and like a lamb before its shearer is silent,
>> so he opens not his mouth.
> In his humiliation justice was denied him.
>> Who can describe his generation?
> For his life is taken away from the earth. (Acts 8:32–33)

The last two phrases are debated: "Who will describe his generation? For his life is taken away from the earth." In the original context, these are laments for the servant's lack of children and his death. But in Acts, they are reversal texts. It is no longer a lamentation but a text that marvels at the incalculable scope of his offspring.

Table 2.2   The Progeny of the Servant and the Eunuch

Text	Isaiah Meaning: Lamentation	Acts Meaning: Exaltation
Who will describe his generation?	No progeny	A myriad of children
For his life is taken from the earth	He is killed	He is raised to life and enthroned

Ultimately, the text is about Jesus, but Jesus is painted in eunuch hues. The joining of the eunuch and the servant is seen in multiple ways. First, two men of means humble themselves and are exalted. Second, they both come before a shearer, or literally, "the one who cut him." This certainly resonates with the eunuch as a castrated male. Third, the "cutting" of both is held in tandem with their progeny.

Jesus is the faithful servant-eunuch who attaches himself not to earthly dynasties or progenies but to God's kingdom. Through forgoing "earthly descendants" and allowing his life to be cut off, Jesus is given heavenly offspring and exalted. His tent curtains are now stretched out.

He is the firstborn of a large family tree (Rom. 8:29; 1 Cor. 15:20, 23; Col. 1:15, 18). He was denied justice, even though he had done nothing wrong. But though justice was denied to him, he is given offspring and exalted. Luke thus communicates that blessing comes through the one who was cut, who was humiliated. Not only that, but the source of the spread of the gospel to Judea and Samaria is Jesus's lifeblood and lifting up.

Jesus is also Savior in Acts (5:31; 13:23). Though the label occurs only twice, related words occur multiple times (4:12; 7:25; 13:26, 47; 16:17; 27:34; 28:28). This paints Jesus as the leader of the people who delivers them from their enemies. He is the King who rescues them.

Jesus is the Son of God (9:20; 13:33), implying he is both King and, even more than that, identified with Yahweh himself. He is the Son of Man whom Stephen sees standing at the right hand of God (7:56). Finally, Jesus is the holy and innocent one (2:27; 3:14; 4:27, 30; 13:35), alluding to the consistent title of Yahweh, the Holy One of Israel, in Isaiah.[d] Luke employs this title to emphasize Jesus's innocence and therefore the aptness of his rising from the dead.

Overall, the characterization of Jesus confirms what we found earlier in this chapter. Jesus was faithful to God's purposes. He was innocent and therefore raised from the dead. He lowered himself and was therefore exalted. He was a faithful eunuch and therefore given many children. He was Son of God and Lord. Now he has been installed as the messianic Son of God and Lord. Jesus died, rose from the grave, and now sits enthroned.

a   Lord (Acts 1:6, 21, 24; 2:20–21, 25, 34, 36, 39, 47; 4:29, 33; 5:9, 14, 19; 7:59–60; 8:16, 22, 24–26, 39; 9:1, 5, 10–11, 13, 15, 17, 27–28, 31, 35, 42; 10:4, 14, 33, 36; 11:8, 16–17, 20–21, 23–24; 12:7, 11, 17, 23; 13:2, 10–12, 44, 47–49; 14:3, 23; 15:11, 17, 26, 35–36, 40; 16:14–15, 30–32; 18:8–9, 25; 19:5, 10, 13, 17, 20; 20:19, 21, 24, 35; 21:13–14; 22:8, 10, 19; 23:11; 26:15; 28:31). Messiah (2:31, 36, 38; 3:6, 18, 20; 4:10, 26; 5:42; 8:5, 12; 9:22, 34; 10:36, 48; 11:17; 15:26; 16:18; 17:3; 18:5, 28; 24:24; 26:23; 28:31).

b   Ben Witherington, *The Acts of the Apostles: A Socio-Rhetorical Commentary* (Grand Rapids, MI: Eerdmans, 1998), 149; emphasis original.

c   Kavin Rowe, "Acts 2.36 and the Continuity of Lukan Christology," *NTS* 53, no. 1 (2007): 55.

d   Isa. 1:4; 5:19; 12:6; 17:7; 29:19; 30:11–15; 31:1; 37:23; 41:14, 16, 20; 43:3, 14; 45:11; 47:4; 48:17; 49:7; 54:5; 60:9, 14.

Conclusion

The Father's plan centralizes on the Son. Acts emphasizes the exaltation of Jesus. Jesus is the risen one who provides life. He is the ascended one who rules. He is Lord and Messiah (Acts 2:36). This is all based on his obedience unto death by which he offers forgiveness of sins. "*Lift up your eyes and see the riches of the / all-sufficient King seated on his throne in glory.*"

Though Jesus is absent bodily in Acts, he is ever present. His resurrection life abounds on the earth. Through his power, the apostles heal, raise the dead, perform miracles, and are released from prison. They proclaim Jesus's new life and offer it to all who are willing to give up their campaigns of death.

In the same way, Christians today are sent out to tell others and spread the presence of new life. Some circles focus only on the "speaking" and others on the "doing," but Acts combines both. Peter preaches

Jesus and heals in his name. Everyone seeks to escape death, whether that be through health care, reputation, or memory. Humans recognize death is a corruption of creation. The message Christians hold forth is one of flourishing, both for now and in the future.

Though Jesus has ascended, his reign is manifested from Jerusalem, to Antioch, to Corinth, to Rome. The apostles can go out declaring the defeat of Satan because of their heavenly ruler. They can press on because he intercedes for them in heaven. They can speak prophetically because he has sent the Spirit after breaking the barrier between heaven and earth.

Modern Christians must remember their King has already been installed on the throne. Christ-followers honor rulers, but they do not pledge their ultimate loyalty to them. Our hope is not found in earthly thrones, but in a heavenly throne that cannot be moved.

Though Jesus's death was recounted in Luke, the ripples spread with increasing force. What the apostles offer is forgiveness of sins. Though Christ was crucified, his blood covers humanity's bloodstained hands. The apostles also embody Christ's death in their own lives as they go about with the aroma of death on their garments. They suffer so that others might live.

Proclaiming the presence of eternal life and an enthroned King might sound triumphalistic. But this must be paired with the fact that life and honor come only through death and shame. Christians carry the aroma of death in their very bodies so that others might live. We must be willing to be shamed so that others might live. We must be willing to follow our suffering servant.

Acts exhibits no absentee Christology. The new era is characterized by the Spirit, but it is the Spirit of Jesus. He is present by the Spirit and through his sanctified. The book is truly the "Acts of the Resurrected and Ascended Lord."[21]

---

21 Thompson, *The Acts of the Risen Lord Jesus.*

The Spirit Empowers

But you will receive power when the
Holy Spirit has come upon you.

ACTS 1:8

Tripping Off the Power

In 2010, Kanye West released a promotional music teaser for his song "Power." The video is more like a live-action photograph. Think of the pictures in Harry Potter, where the people in the images move. The camera slowly zooms out on Kanye.

He is standing in the middle with a black shirt, surrounded by people, and a large gold chain is draped around his neck. His placement in the center of the image indicates his power, and behind him is a never-ending row of pillars. The row of pillars represents Kanye's palace, temple, or throne.

Kanye raps about his superhuman power; he was consistently at the top of music charts. Likewise, a king without power is no king at all. Kanye can speak of his power only because there is evidence of it. A temple so to speak.

In Acts, evidence of God's power exists as well. God's power is connected to Jesus's sacrificial and victorious kingship. But by the twelfth verse of Acts, Jesus is gone. His body has ascended to the heavens. So how does his rule reach the earth?

Jesus's power is not embodied in earthly thrones or gold chains but through the work of his Spirit, who crafts his new temple. The Spirit is the matchmaker between heaven and earth.

Chrysostom says, "The Gospels are a history of what Christ did and said; but Acts, of what that 'other Comforter' said and did." He also calls Acts "the Polity of the Holy Spirit."[1] While other literature in the New Testament interprets the work of the Spirit, Acts recounts the work of the Spirit in history.[2]

Though some point to the work of the Spirit as the main theological theme in Acts, this theme logically comes *under* and *after* the Father's plan and the life and reign of the ascended Lord. In other words, Pneumatology (Spirit) must be connected to Patriology (Father) and Christology (Son). This ordering is evidenced in a number of ways in Acts.

Jesus speaks of the Spirit as the *Father's promise* (Luke 24:49; Acts 1:4; 2:33, 39). The sending of the Spirit was the Father's design. The Spirit enacts God's plan. Historically, it has been affirmed the Spirit *spirates* from the Father and Son.[3] The Spirit, therefore, proceeds from the divine will of the Father.

Christ's ascent must also precede the arrival of the Spirit. As Elijah's mantle fell to Elisha in his ascent, so the Spirit descended after the ascension of Christ. As Peter says, "Being therefore exalted at the right hand of God, and having received from the Father the promise of the Holy Spirit, he has poured out this that you yourselves are seeing and hearing" (Acts 2:33).

The Spirit's work, therefore, cannot be separated from the one who bestows the Spirit. The Old Testament promised that the king from David's line would have the Spirit (Isa. 11:2; 42:1). In Jesus's mission statement in Luke 4:18–19 (Isa. 61:1–2), he says,

---

1 Chrysostom, Homily 1 on Acts, in *NPNF*, Series 1, vol. 11, ed. Philip Schaff (Grand Rapids, MI: Eerdmans, 1925), 7; Homily 2, 18.

2 Daniel Marguerat, *The First Christian Historian: Writing the "Acts of the Apostles,"* trans. Ken McKinney, Gregory J. Laughery, and Richard Bauckham (Cambridge: Cambridge University Press, 2002), 109–10.

3 This language of spiration comes from the Gospel of John, where Jesus breathes on the disciples and they receive the Spirit (John 20:22).

The Spirit of the Lord is on me,

because he has anointed me

to proclaim good news to the poor.

He has sent me to proclaim liberty to the captives

and recovering of sight to the blind,

to set at liberty those who are oppressed,

to proclaim the year of the Lord's favor.

Acts continues this story but transitions to a new stage after Christ's ascension—now the Spirit rests on his people as it rested on him. The Spirit testifies to Christ, and Christ testifies to the Father. If God is the writer of Acts, Jesus is the director, and the Spirit is the main actor. This is why the Spirit receives so much attention in Acts. He is the one on the stage enacting release to the captives.

The work of the Spirit is therefore vital to any reading of Acts, but in narrative order. The Father's plan is prior, and so is Christ's exaltation. This chapter looks at the Spirit from three perspectives in Acts: soteriological, ecclesiological, and missiological.

Many speak only of the Spirit's work as related to mission following the key statement in Acts 1:8. However, it is better to speak of the empowering of the Spirit in Acts, an empowering with three distinct but related facets. The Spirit is about mission, but the mission is to save, recreate, and reconcile a new people.

Table 3.1   The Spirit Empowers

Soteriological	The Spirit applies Christ's salvation at Pentecost and beyond.
Ecclesiological	The Spirit creates a new people at Pentecost and beyond.
Missiological	The Spirit propels his people to testify Christ to the world.

The Spirit and Salvation

While we can and should speak about the Spirit in relation to mission, Luke actually starts with the Spirit's restoration, renewal, cleansing, liberating, and transforming work.[4] The Spirit is the presence of God and therefore bestows salvation.

As theologians have stated throughout the centuries, the Spirit applies salvation. The Gospel of Luke appropriately precedes Acts. Jesus accomplishes salvation through the cross and resurrection. Jesus's blood defeats the powers of darkness and blots out the sin of mankind. In this sense, salvation is accomplished in Luke. However, the Spirit is still involved with salvation. Their operations are inseperable.

In Acts 2, the outpouring of the Spirit leads people to call upon the name of the Lord for salvation (Acts 2:21; cf. Joel 2:32). Readers should note the progression: salvation comes by means of confessing Christ, but this comes about *when* the Spirit is poured out on all flesh (Acts 2:17). The Spirit draws people to Jesus and also joins them to him, thereby applying salvation.

The salvific and missional realities of the Spirit are connected but also distinct. Salvation logically *preeceds* mission. People can't go out until they come in. People can't be sent until they are called. One can see this progression as one looks at the narrative order of Luke's second volume. Acts 2 and Pentecost become the generative core of the rest of the narrative.

The Spirit must fall from on high before the apostles set out on mission (Acts 2). Though they receive the commission before Pentecost, the mission doesn't begin until the Spirit comes. Even before the commission, Jesus told to them stay in Jerusalem until they were baptized from on high (Luke 24:49). They don't have the power to go out until the Spirit arrives.

This "from on high" language evokes Isaiah 32:15 and the hopes of the restoration of Israel (Isa. 32:15–20). To be restored is another way of speaking of salvation. As the Old Testament promised, Israel was always meant to be a blessing to the nations, but to do so, they needed the cleansing and empowering presence of the Spirit. The Torah needed to be applied to their hearts.

---

4   Max Turner, *Power from on High: The Spirit in Israel's Restoration and Witness in Luke-Acts* (Sheffield: Sheffield Academic Press, 1996), 186. Ultimately, the two (sanctification and evangelism) cannot be separated.

Pentecost, through the use of numerous allusions, indicates that Jesus's disciples become the restored Israel and mobile temple community. *The Spirit restores by bringing the presence of God to earth.* The imagery in Acts 2 gives evidence of God's saving presence.

Fire and wind descend. Both indicate the people are the new temple, the place where the presence of God resides. Wind in the Old Testament refers to God's presence. The glory cloud would fill the temple or tabernacle, indicating it was God's dwelling place (Ex. 40:35; 1 Kings 8:11; 2 Chron. 7:2; Isa. 6:4; Ezek. 10:4). The presence of God also established his people (Ex. 25:21–22; Lev. 16:2; Num. 9:18–23; 1 Kings 8:10–13; Ezek. 10).[5] The Spirit (wind), from the beginning, was the one who gave life, who breathed the breath of God into human beings and brought order out chaos (cf. Gen. 1:2). Wind cannot be controlled, but its presence is felt (John 3:8). It therefore indicates the sovereign, untamed, and active work of God.

Fire likewise points to the temple. God revealed himself not only as wind but also as fire. He appeared as a smoking fire pot (Gen. 15:17), in the burning bush to Moses (Ex. 3:2), a pillar of fire at night to the wilderness generation (Ex. 13:21), on Mount Sinai as smoke and fire (Ex. 19:18; 24:17; Heb. 12:18–21).

Fire was also associated with the temple as Israel offered sacrifices (Ex. 29:18) and fire burned inside the tabernacle (Ex. 40:38) and temple (2 Chron. 7:1; 1 Enoch 14:8–25).[6] God answers in fire on Mount Carmel (1 Kings 18:38), and when Elijah requests help (2 Kings 1:12). Fire, like wind, indicates the presence of God, but it was also a form of judgment (Lev. 10:2; Num. 16:35; Job 1:16; 2 Kings 1:9–12).

---

5   Beale notes the theophany at Babel manifested strong wind according to Josephus (*Ant.* 1.118; *Sibylline Oracles* 3:101–02). At Babel the people attempted to build a temple, but now God was completing that act by coming down, not them coming up to him. G. K. Beale, *The Temple and the Church's Mission: A Biblical Theology of the Dwelling Place of God*, NSBT (Downers Grove, IL: IVP, 2004), 202–5.

6   The Dead Sea Scrolls (1Q29) say the Urim and Thummin stones, which were placed on the high priest's breastplate (Ex. 28:30) shone with "tongues of fire." The people are now the new high priests and indicate the Spirit brings the holy of holies to them.

At Pentecost, the fire divides and does not consume. It comes not on the mountain but rests on people rather than annihilating them.[7] Here, the fire is more personal, as it divides over each of them, indicating they are now filled with the presence of God individually and corporately. In the Old Testament, people are not fit for the fire of God to dwell on them, but now they have the ascended priest interceding for them and pleading their case and thereby become priestly prophets like Moses.

When Jesus tells his disciples to wait at Jerusalem, they are waiting for the empowering of the Spirit. However, this empowering is not only for mission but also for renewal, restoration, salvation. Though the apostles believed in Jesus before, the new covenant promises are applied at Pentecost. The Spirit remakes them, he renews their hearts, before they go out to the ends of the earth.

As the narrative of Acts continues, the work of the Spirit also restores Gentiles (cf. Acts 10–11; 13:52; 15:8). Gentiles throughout Acts receive the gift of the Spirit (10:46–47), and when the apostles see it, they cannot deny that the Gentiles are followers of Jesus. The Spirit unifies and purifies not only Israel, therefore, but all people under the reign of Jesus.

The Spirit and the Church

The Spirit's work in Acts is soteriological, but the Spirit also assembles, shapes, and strengthens a new community to follow its messianic King (ecclesiological).[8] In Acts, the emphasis is not so much on the individual experience of the Spirit but on the *corporate reception* of the Spirit and *corporate creation* by the Spirit.

God saved a people in Exodus by blood and the splitting of waters. He shaped them as his covenant people at Sinai by giving them the Torah. The same pattern appears in Luke-Acts. Jesus redeemed people by his blood; the Spirit applies the Torah to the hearts of the people, forming a new community.

---

7   This is similar to the burning bush where the fire does not consume the bush.

8   Turner, *Power from on High*, 415.

The corporate nature of Acts 2 is clear by the timestamp: Pentecost. Time is liturgical for Israel. *When* something happens is as important as *what* happens. Three pilgrimage feasts existed for Israel. Passover was a time to remember redemption from Egypt (Ex. 12; Lev. 23:4–8; Num. 9; Deut. 16; Ezek. 45). The feast of ingathering (Pentecost) looked back to God's provision for his people at Sinai (Lev. 23:9–14). The Feast of Booths reminded Israel of God dwelling with his people in the tent in their wilderness wanderings.

Table 3.2   The Rhythm and Typology of Jewish Feasts

Jewish Pilgrimage Feasts	Event	Jesus and the Church
Passover (Unleaved Bread)	The Exodus	Death/Burial of Jesus
Pentecost (Weeks)	Sinai	Descent of the Spirit
Booths (Tabernacles or Tents)	Wilderness Wandering	Dwelling with his People (Lev. 23:40) Remembering the Law (Deut. 31:10–13) All nations welcomed (Zech. 14)

In Jewish tradition, the feast of ingathering (Ex. 23:16; Deut. 16:9–12) was tightly tied to Sinai, coming between the Passover and the Feast of Booths.[9] It was an agricultural festival acknowledging God's abundant provision on the earth. It had become the day to celebrate Moses's receiving of the Torah on Mount Sinai.

The feast was called *Pentecost* ("fifty") in Greek, following the historical account in Exodus 19:1–3 of Israel's arrival at Sinai fifty days after the Passover. Therefore, the Spirit comes at Pentecost to fulfill Sinai and reconstitute the people of God (Isa. 44:1–4).

Pentecost was also a festival in which the exiles of Israel gathered together, further illustrating the ecclesiological function of the Spirit. God

9   See Goulder's and Turner's arguments for the tie between Pentecost and Sinai. M. D. Goulder, *Type and History in Acts* (London: SPCK, 1964), 149–52; Turner, *Power from on High*, 280–82.

had promised he would bring his offspring from the east, west, north, and south (Acts 2:9–11; Isa. 43:5–7; Deut. 30:1–10; Isa. 56:8; 60:4; 66:20).

This gathering as God's recongregated people is seen in Acts 2:9–11 as Luke catalogues the people visiting from diverse regions:

> Parthians and Medes and Elamites and residents of Mesopotamia, Judea and Cappadocia, Pontus and Asia, Phrygia and Pamphylia, Egypt and the parts of Libya belonging to Cyrene, and visitors from Rome, both Jews and proselytes, Cretans and Arabians.

Zephaniah tells of the day when the Lord will gather his people and bring them home (Zeph. 3:20). The updated table of nations reflects different directions with Jerusalem at the center.

Figure 3.1   The Ingathering of Exiles at Pentecost

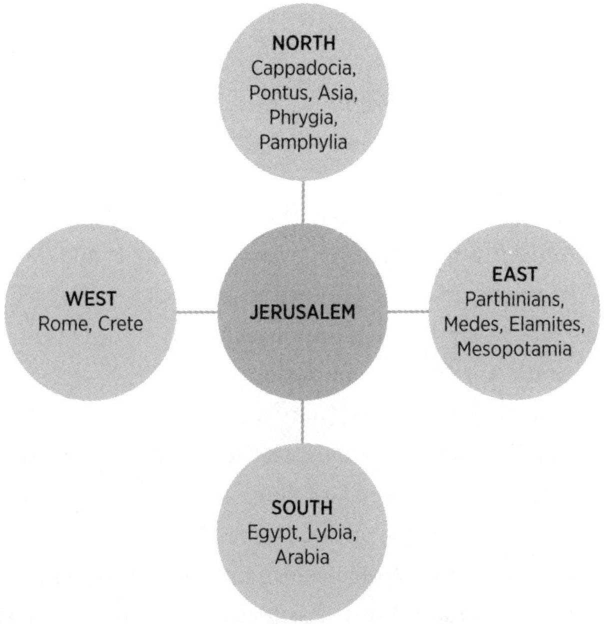

The exiles who reside in all nations are being regathered as Isaiah predicted:

In that day the Lord will extend his hand yet a second time to recover the remnant that remains of his people, from Assyria, from Egypt, from Pathros, from Cush, from Elam, from Shinar, from Hamath, and from the coastlands of the sea.

> He will raise a signal for the nations
>> and will assemble the banished of Israel,
> and gather the dispersed of Judah
>> from the four corners of the earth. (Isa. 11:11–12)

> Fear not, for I am with you;
>> I will bring your offspring from the east,
>> and from the west I will gather you.
> I will say to the north, Give up,
>> and to the south, Do not withhold;
> bring my sons from afar
>> and my daughters from the end of the earth,
> everyone who is called by my name,
>> whom I created for my glory,
>> whom I formed and made. (Isa. 43:5–7)

The parallels with Mount Sinai, therefore, go beyond the calendar rhythm. At Pentecost, this regathered Israel held a "sacred assembly" and offered a pleasing aroma to the Lord (Num. 28:26–27 CSB). This phrase "sacred assembly" is reminiscent of when God called his people to be a kingdom of priests and a holy nation (Ex. 19:3–6). At Mount Sinai, all Israel also gathered together, Moses ascended the mountain, the Lord descended in fire, a great storm surrounded Sinai, and the law was given to Moses so that Israel could be a kingdom of priests.

Additionally, at Pentecost three thousand people are saved. If Pentecost alludes to the Sinai tradition, then the three thousand that die in Exodus 32:28 are remade here as the people respond to Peter's message. The Spirit brings life where the law brought death. Judas's fate was in the desolate place, but the Spirit will make desolate places into gardens (Isa. 32:15; Ezek. 36:35).

Finally, at Pentecost the people gathered by the Spirit devote themselves to teaching, fellowship, prayer, breaking of bread, and generosity (Acts 2:42–47; 4:32). These descriptions mirror what the Torah community were called to do. Deuteronomy 15:1–4 specifically calls them to cancel debts and not have anyone poor among them. Luke indicates the people who heard Peter's Pentecost sermon are the new covenant community and the true followers of the Torah. In a time when the rich controlled most of the wealth, they share their goods with one another and provide for the needy (Acts 2:42–47; 4:32–37; 6:1–7). The Spirit is intimately involved with the economic practices of the early church. He compels the people to share their resources with one another and provide for the poor. One mark of the Spirit's work, one mark of a true church, is generosity to the needy.

As argued above, the Pentecost-Sinai parallels are abundant: the people gather as a sacred assembly according to the Sinai rhythm, fire and wind appear, three thousand are saved, and the community fulfills the Torah's ideal. Through these parallels, Luke indicates this is a regathering, a new covenant ceremony, a sprinkling of blood, a creation of a new people after God's heart. Erasmus makes much of the Pentecost connection with Sinai:

> On the mountain the Old Law was given, written on tablets of stone;
> in an upper room the New Law was given, written by the Holy Spirit.
> . . . In both cases, an elevated place, in both cases, fire.[10]

In the next section, we will consider how the Spirit also expands this community beyond Israel to the nations. Salvation, community, and mission all are interrelated.

The Spirit and Mission

Though I have withheld the theme up to this point, the Spirit does empower for mission in Acts. Luke says that when the Spirit comes,

---

10 Desiderius Erasmus, *Paraphrase on Acts*, trans. Robert D. Sider, vol. 50 of *Collected Works of Erasmus* (Toronto: University of Toronto Press, 1995), 13–14.

the apostles will be witnesses (Acts 1:8), they will prophesy (2:17–18), and declare God's message (2:4; 4:8, 31; 6:10; 9:17–20; 13:9–11). The Spirit not only saves and establishes the church but also empowers it for cross-cultural evangelism (8:29; 10:19–20; 13:2, 4; 15:28).

The Spirit overcomes natural impulses to forbid the incorporation of the "other." He joins diverse groups together.[11] Orchestrating cross-cultural encounters and affirming a common status for all indwelt believers, the Spirit becomes a "central figure in the formation of a new social identity that affirms yet chastens and transcends ethnic identity."[12]

The Spirit compels his witnesses to go to Samaria and the ends of the earth. The Spirit was promised to empower witnesses for the Gentile mission (1:8), enacted a unified voice at Pentecost (2:4), performed wonders through Philip in Samaria (8:6–7), directed Philip to the eunuch (8:29), led Peter to Cornelius (11:12), confirmed Cornelius's status (10:44), and made a decision at the Jerusalem council about the Gentiles acceptance (15:28–29).

As Keener says, "the same Spirit has led the Jerusalem church to a theology that welcomes Gentiles."[13] The Spirit continues to propel Paul to the nations as he welcomes Gentiles. The church's ongoing life of love, acceptance, and generosity is dependent on the Spirit.

This is all based on the power the Spirit gives to his people as declared in Acts 1:8 and narrated in Acts 2. But what sort of power does he give the apostles? The specific *dynamis* (power) they have is not the power of an army or an expert. Power in Acts coincides with word-deed ministries that testify to life and hospitality found in Jesus and his new community.

For example, in 4:7, after Peter has healed the lame man, the leaders ask, "By what *power* or by what name did you do this?" They raised the lame man and welcomed him into the community by the power of the

11 Aaron J. Kuecker, *The Spirit and the "Other": Social Identity, Ethnicity and Intergroup Reconciliation in Luke-Acts*, LNTS 444 (London: Bloomsbury T&T Clark, 2011), 168.

12 Kuecker, *The Spirit and the "Other*," 216.

13 Craig S. Keener, *Acts: An Exegetical Commentary*, vol. 3, *15:1–23:35* (Grand Rapids, MI: Baker Academic, 2012), 2291.

Spirit. He crossed temple boundaries in this event and was welcomed into the temple community.

Then 4:33 says, "And with great *power* the apostles were giving their testimony to the resurrection of the Lord Jesus." And in 6:8, "And Stephen, full of grace and *power*, was doing great wonders and signs among the people" (cf. 8:13; 10:38; 19:11). In all this, the Spirit's power is tied to salvation in Jesus and community in Jesus.

This is further supported throughout Acts as the Spirit gives "boldness" to people as they speak of Christ. Boldness and the Spirit are interwoven. Peter speaks with "confidence/boldness" about the Messiah's resurrection (2:29). Peter and John have boldness when they proclaim the death and exaltation of Jesus as the power behind their raising the lame man to walk (4:13). The apostles continue to ask for boldness in the face of persecution and are immediately answered (4:29–31).

Early in his ministry, Paul preaches boldly in the name of Jesus (9:27–28). In their first mission, Paul and Barnabas speak boldly to those in Pisidian Antioch and Iconium about the life found in Jesus (13:46; 14:3). In Ephesus, Paul enters the synagogue and speaks boldly about the kingdom of God (19:8). To Agrippa, Paul speaks boldly (26:26), and to those in Rome, he declares Christ with boldness (28:31).

The scope of this mission is outlined in Acts 1:8: Jerusalem, Judea and Samaria, and the ends of the earth. A distinctly geographical presentation of the spread of the good news exists in Acts, and the order is important. The blessings to the nations will come forth from Jerusalem because God promised Abraham his children would bless the nations (Gen. 12:3; Isa. 49:6; Acts 13:47).

Conclusion

The world's definition of power stands in contrast to God's. Worldly power has to do with capacity or ability to direct and influence behavior. In one way, this is similar to the Spirit's power. He also directs and influences behavior. However, worldly power is usually employed for selfish reasons.

In contrast, the Spirit's power allows people to testify to the exalted King. The Spirit's power makes people whole by making them others-centered. The Spirit's power compels people to welcome people they usually would not and share with those in need. The Spirit's power pushes people into persecution. In Acts, people are constantly catching up with the Spirit's work as he leads them.

Therefore, the Spirit empowers in Acts. He brings the benefits of Christ from heaven to earth. While many look at the Spirit's work primarily in terms of mission, the Spirit also has a soteriological and ecclesiological function. These three (soteriological, ecclesiological, and missiological) cannot be separated. However, they can and should be distinguished.

Though Jesus gives his commission at the beginning of Acts (1:8), the apostles must wait in Jerusalem until the Spirit comes and restores them. At Pentecost, he comes as wind and fire, indicating the presence of God is with them and thus applying Christ's sacrifice to them (soteriological).

The people of God are also regathered and remade at Pentecost. Jews gather from all nations, and the effect of the Spirit is to create a new people (ecclesiological). The Spirit empowers this new Torah community to go to the nations with words that testify to Jesus and deeds that imitate him (missiological).

Not surprisingly, the narrative progression of Luke-Acts follows the pattern found in the Pentateuch. Israel is redeemed by blood and brought out of Egypt. God meets with his people on a high place and establishes a new covenant community. They are then called to be a light to the nations by their distinct lives.

In Luke's retelling, each element of the familiar story is amplified. Jesus's blood is better than the blood on the doorposts. The Spirit's presence is better than that at the tabernacle. And the mission to the ends of the earth is directed by God himself.

As Sarah Coakley affirms, the Spirit can't be reduced from the powerful brooding Dove, to a "shrinking Pigeon—small, shadowy, and hard to see."[14] The Spirit is ever-active in Acts, testifying to Jesus and effecting the Father's plan.

If believers have been sealed with the same Spirit, then this mission continues. The story of God's plan did not stop at Acts 28. It continues in those who confess Jesus, share their resources, and spread Jesus's name with boldness.

---

14 Sarah Coakley, *God, Sexuality, and the Self: An Essay "On the Trinity"* (Cambridge: Cambridge University Press, 2013), 212.

The Word Multiplies

So the word of the Lord continued to
increase and prevail mightily.

ACTS 19:20

The Word as a Divine Actor

As I noted at the beginning of this book, many propose different "central" theological themes of Acts. Most claim it is the Spirit, while others say it is the apostles or Jesus himself. More recent proposals focus on the word. For example, David Peterson's commentary on Acts helpfully highlights the importance of the word as almost a divine character in the book of Acts. He argues,

> The real hero of Acts is the *logos*, the Word. . . . The ascended Lord Jesus
> is the central figure in the narrative, and he employs his word and his
> Spirit to advance his purpose through human agents in the world."[1]

It is true, the word becomes an actor on the stage of Acts. To put this another way, the word is tightly connected to *the Word*. Like in

[1] David G. Peterson, *The Acts of the Apostles*, PNTC (Grand Rapids, MI: Eerdmans, 2009), 33.

the rest of the Bible, the word creates, sustains, and grows. The word is a divine actor in Acts and the Scriptures as a whole.

However, the centrality of the word in Acts can be seen not only in the explicit emphasis on this theme but also in the form in which Acts was written. About one third of Acts is comprised of speeches or evangelistic preaching.

The centrality of the evangelistic sermons by Peter (Acts 2:14–36, 38–39; 3:12–26; 4:8–12; 10:34–43), Paul (13:16–41; 14:3–7; 17:22–34; 20:17–35; 22:1–21; 23:1–6; 24:10–21; 26:2–23; 28:17–20), and a few other characters (7; 8:5; 15:13–21) contributes to the literary structure and not only paces the narrative but embodies one of Luke's major themes.

These speeches thus demonstrate one of Luke's emphases: the progress of the word. Peter preaches largely in Jerusalem, the Hellenistic servants spread the word in Judea and Samaria, and Paul proclaims the good news to the ends of the earth among the Gentiles. Luke makes this progress explicit by including summary statements of the multiplication in 6:7; 9:31; 12:24; 16:5; 19:20; 28:30–31.

Table 4.1   Texts on the Growth of the Church

6:7	And the word of God continued to increase, and the number of the disciples multiplied greatly in Jerusalem, and a great many of the priests became obedient to the faith.
9:31	So the church throughout all Judea and Galilee and Samaria had peace and was being built up. And walking in the fear of the Lord and in the comfort of the Holy Spirit, it multiplied.
12:24	But the word of God increased and multiplied.
16:5	So the churches were strengthened in the faith, and they increased in numbers daily.
19:20	So the word of the Lord continued to increase and prevail mightily.
28:30–31	He lived there two whole years at his own expense, and welcomed all who came to him, proclaiming the kingdom of God and teaching about the Lord Jesus Christ with all boldness and without hindrance.

Three sections will be covered in this chapter: the Trinity and the word, the content of the word, and the multiplication of the word. The theme of "the word" is ever present in Acts. However, it must be put in narrative and logical order. The word progresses according to the plan of the Father, testifying to the exalted Son, and in the power of the Spirit. The Trinitarian shape has priority.

Table 4.2   The Word Multiplies

The Trinity	The Father directs the word, the message concerns the Son, and it is empowered by the Spirit.
Content	The good news of the kingdom found in King Jesus.
Multiplication	The word becomes a divine character in Acts that conquers and has an active force.

The Trinity and the Word

In Acts, the word has a Trinitarian shape. The Spirit empowers people to speak the word of God about the risen and exalted Christ. The Trinitarian nature of this formula is hard to miss. The word is allied to the Father, Son, and Spirit.

In Acts, the Father is ultimately responsible for the expansion of the word; he directs and enables his messengers through the power of the Spirit (13:47; 14:27; 15:12; 28:28). Not surprisingly, Luke's favorite modifier for the word is "of God" which should most likely be taken as a possessive modifier. It is God's word. He is the owner, proprietor, and administrator of the word.

A quick survey of the "word of God" in Acts reveals that almost every major section has a reference. The "word of God" emerges in Jerusalem (4:31), Judea (6:2, 7), Samaria (8:14), and the ends of the earth (11:1; 12:24; 13:5, 7, 46; 17:13; 18:11). This includes the encounter with Cornelius (11:1), the conclusion of the first half of Acts (12:24), the first missionary journey (13:5, 7, 46), the second journey (17:13), and the third journey (18:11). Whether this was intentional on Luke's part is hard to tell, but the prominence of the "word of God" certainly spans the scope of Acts.

The word is not only the Father's and spreads at his direction but also coupled to Christ the Son. While this topic will be covered in more detail in the next section, it should be noted here that God's messengers testify to the life, death, resurrection, and enthronement of the Son. The word concerns the Son. He is the content and the subject of the word.

Luke modifies the word not only with "of God" but also with "of the Lord." This is his second favorite appellation (8:25; 11:16; 13:44, 48, 49; 15:35–36; 16:32; 19:10, 20; 20:35). In Acts, *kyrios* especially refers to Christ (2:36). Again, the phrase is likely possessive, meaning the Lord's word. But it could also be a more ambiguous genitive, meaning the Lord is the author and content of the word.

Finally, the Spirit works in concert with the word. If the Father is the proprietor of the word and Christ is the content, then the Spirit is the energy behind the word. The Spirit empowers Yahweh's people to speak the word.

Joel connects the coming of the Spirit to prophesying (Joel 2:28). Throughout Acts, when the Spirit comes people speak in tongues. As Thompson explains, "The link between the enablement of the Spirit and the ability to speak for God is highlighted throughout Acts with the word *pimplemi* (filled) followed by an activity of speaking."[2]

- In Acts 2:4, the apostles are filled with the Spirit and begin to speak.
- In Acts 4:31, at a prayer meeting, the apostles are filled with the Holy Spirit and speak the word of God boldly.
- In Acts 6:10, the Spirit enables Stephen to speak.
- In Acts 9:17–20, Saul is filled with the Spirit and he begins to preach in the synagogues.
- In Acts 13:9–11, Paul is filled with the Holy Spirit and pronounces judgment.

2   Alan Thompson, *The Acts of the Risen Lord Jesus: Luke's Account of God's Unfolding Plan*, NSBT (Downers Grove, IL: InterVarsity Press, 2011), 133. The eschatological coming of the Spirit is described by Luke as clothing, baptism, coming upon, falling upon, pouring out, reception, and filling. These metaphors are complementary, and interpreters should not give more weight to one than the others.

The Spirit compels speech about the word. However, the Spirit also confirms the reception of the word and applies its welcome (1:8; 2:3, 38; 5:32; 6:1–3; 7:51; 8:16–17, 39–40; 9:17; 10:45; 11:12, 15–16; 15:8; 11:24; 13:1–2). Word and the Spirit are like the sun and its rays—the two exist together.

The Trinitarian shape of the word is reiterated in the book's final verse: "[Paul was] proclaiming the kingdom of God and teaching about the Lord Jesus Christ with all boldness and without hindrance" (28:31). He was preaching (1) the kingdom of *God*, (2) the *Lord Jesus Christ*, and (3) these with all *boldness* and without hindrance. Paul's message concerns God's plan, centering on the Son, by the power of the Spirit.

Table 4.3   Trinitarian Preaching in Acts 28:31

Father	Proclaiming the kingdom of God
Son	Teaching about the Lord Jesus Christ
Spirit	With all boldness

In summary, the Father directs the spread of the word; it is his word. But the word also is centered on the Son. That is why it is also called the "word of the Lord." The Spirit empowers God's people to speak the words of God with all boldness. God creates worlds with words in Acts. He commands his people to join him in spreading the gospel with the declaration of Jesus as Lord.

The Content of the Word

If the word has a Trinitarian shape, the content of the word has a Christological center. The Spirit fills people and causes them to preach the word about Christ. Two main synonyms are used in Acts that inform readers concerning the content of the word: the gospel and the message of the kingdom. Both of these show Jesus is the subject of the Word.

While the noun "gospel" rarely appears in Acts (Acts 15:7; 20:24) the related verb "evangelize" or "preach the gospel" occurs extensively.

The object of "evangelizing" in Acts is the word (8:4; 15:35), Christ Jesus (5:42; 8:35; 11:20; 17:18), the kingdom (8:12), peace (10:36), the promise (13:32), or sometimes the content is simply assumed (8:25, 40; 14:7, 15, 21; 16:10). What then, exactly, does it mean "to gospelize"?

Euaggelion (gospel) is a media term—a message of good news, a dispatch of victory, and the term is traditionally employed in political contexts. Luke adopts this political sense, but he also clarifies and reconfigures it, largely following the lead of the prophet Isaiah.

According to Isaiah, the good news is that Yahweh reigns through his servant's suffering and exaltation. Isaiah uses the term "gospel" in relationship to the coming reign of Yahweh and the return from exile. Zion and Jerusalem are to proclaim the "good news" of God's return to establish his rule, which is further described as Yahweh shepherding his people (Isa. 40:9–11).

The prophet also declares that the bloodied and dusty feet of those who carry good news are beautiful because they proclaim peace and salvation, and announce that God reigns (Isa. 52:7). Isaiah 52:7 parallels the good news with God's reign, which brings peace and salvation.

In Isaiah 61:1, the anointed one announces the Spirit of Yahweh is upon him to bring good news, which is further defined as proclaiming liberty to the captives, recovery of sight to the blind, and setting at liberty those who are oppressed (cf. Luke 4:18–19).

This is Luke's focus. The word concerns the good news for those who are captive and bound. It is for the lame man who is stuck outside the temple (Acts 3–4). It is for the eunuch who cannot enter the temple (Acts 8). It is for Samaritans who worship at another temple. It is for barbarians who are uncultured (Acts 28).

In Acts, like Isaiah, the scope of the good news is not only for Israel but for the whole world (1:8). Acts is about the spread of this "word" to various regions and people groups. The apostles preach the gospel in Jerusalem (5:42), in Samaria (8:4, 12, 25), on the desert road (8:35), in the coastal cities (8:40), in Caesarea (10:36) and Antioch (11:20) and Asia Minor (13:32; 14:7, 15, 21), and in Macedonia and Achaia (16:10; 17:18).

In Acts, the primary opposition is not Rome or any other foreign nation, but sin, death, the world, and Satan, who work through flesh and blood, especially in the killing of Jesus (2:38; 3:19; 5:31; 7:60; 8:22; 10:43; 13:38; 17:30; 22:16; 26:18–20). What the nations need is forgiveness of sins. What they need is the power of the Spirit to change their hearts.

The means by which the good news is accomplished is not by sword or armies but by the suffering of the servant and his servants. As many have noted, suffering in Acts provides an opportunity for more ministry and catapults the word forward. Scott Cunningham even states that "persecution is an almost omnipresent plot device" in Acts.[3]

Yet the content of the gospel for Luke is the same as it is for Isaiah: the suffering and exalted servant. The apostles preach the King and his kingdom. They preach Jesus as the Messiah (5:42; 8:35; 10:36; 11:20; 17:18; 28:31), the kingdom of God (8:12; 19:8; 20:25; 28:23; 28:31), the promise of Jesus (13:32), and the reality of the living God (14:15).

The content of this word is therefore about Christ the King and those he welcomes into his kingdom. The apostles proclaim that the age of fulfillment has dawned through Jesus's work.

The Multiplication of the Word

In Acts, the word has a Trinitarian shape and a Christological center. If the triune God is behind it and the message concerns Christ, there is no impeding it. It will conquer, progress, and multiply. The word has an active force in Acts.

Luke's characterization of the word is not new to him. A biblical theology supports this type of reading as the word becomes a divine character. The word is the *agent* of creation, the new exodus, and the kingdom. In Genesis, God creates by his word (Gen. 1:3; John 1:1). In Isaiah, his word doesn't return to him void (Isa. 2:3; 55:10–13). In the Gospels, God's word in Jesus grows and spreads (Mark 4:3–23).

---

3 Scott Cunningham, *Through Many Tribulations: The Theology of Persecution in Luke-Acts*, JSNTSS 142 (Sheffield, UK: Sheffield Academic, 1997), 287; cf. chap. 4, 337–38.

Peterson helpfully summarizes the importance of this concept:

> In Scripture, "the word of God" is viewed as a vital force, reaching into people's lives and transforming situations according to God's will (e.g., Isa 2:3; 55:10–13; Jer 23:28–29; Rom 1:16; 10:17–18; 1 Thess 2:13; Heb 4:12–13; 1 Pet 1:23–25). Jesus' parable of the soils (Luke 8:4–15) was probably particularly in Luke's mind, with its encouragement that the seed of the gospel which fell on good ground "came up and yielded a crop, a hundred times more than was sown" (Luke 8:8). Thus, Luke coined an expression which means that the church which is the creature of the word grew.[4]

In Acts, the word continues to be the agent of the new creation: growing, conquering, and acting with power. It is strange to speak about the word *growing*. Words are not animate beings that grow. Living things propagate. But the word in the Bible is living because it is closely connected to the triune God.

Luke picks up on this theme in Acts. This can be seen throughout the book, but three parallel references (6:7; 12:24; 19:20) have the specific language. All of them refer to the word growing, multiplying, and increasing. All of these phrases paint the church as the new exodus generation that multiplies despite hardship (Ex. 1:7; 20). Francois Bovon concludes that Acts "narrates the diffusion of the word."[5]

Table 4.4   The Multiplication of the Word in Acts

6:7	And the word of God continued to increase, and the number of the disciples *multiplied* greatly in Jerusalem, and a great many of the priests became obedient to the faith.
12:24	But the word of God increased and *multiplied*.
19:20	So the word of the Lord continued to *increase* and prevail mightily.

4   Peterson, *The Acts of the Apostles*, 236.
5   Francois Bovon, *Luke the Theologian: Thirty-Three Years of Research (1950–1983)*, trans. Ken McKinney, PTMS 12 (Allison Park, PA: Pickwick, 1987), 238.

In the section about the Hellenistic widows, the twelve say they need to appoint servants since it is not right for them to give up preaching the word of God to serve tables (Acts 6:2, 4). The result of this administrative decision is the word of God continues to grow, and the number of disciples increases greatly (6:7). Satan seeks to squelch growth by having cultural differences divide them, but God leads them to unity, which furthers advancement.

In Acts 12, Herod kills James and puts Peter in prison. However, an angel of the Lord releases Peter and then strikes Herod down for making himself a god. Forces of the state seek to bind the growth of the word, but after Peter's release, Luke says the word of God increased and multiplied (12:24).

In Acts 19, Paul is in Ephesus dealing with magical practices and the Artemis cult. Paul is portrayed as a mighty miracle worker, and some seek to use this power for their own advancement, but a reverse exorcism occurs, showing the power of God. Magicians therefore recognize a new power has come to the earth and they burn their books, and Luke says the word of the Lord continued to increase and prevail mightily (19:20).

In each text, the word multiplies in the midst of opposition.[6] This theme continues throughout Acts as a whole. The first appearance of "word" occurs in Acts 4:4 in Jerusalem where it states many believed the word and the number of men came to about five thousand. However, the immediately preceding verse pairs this growth with Peter and John's incarceration (4:3).

In 4:29, the apostles pray in the midst of persecution that they might be able speak the word with boldness. In Acts 8, those who are being scattered because of Stephen's persecution proclaim the word (8:4). As Paul travels to Cyprus, he and Barnabas proclaim the word of God in the synagogues of the Jews (13:5) but will later face opposition.

The word also prevails as a proconsul comes to faith (13:12). In Pisidian Antioch, Paul and Barnabas proclaim the word of this salvation to Jews

---

6 David W. Pao, *Acts and the Isaianic New Exodus* (Eugene, OR: Wipf & Stock, 2016), 150.

(13:26), but are then rebuffed by them, and when the Gentiles hear the word is for them, they praise the word of the Lord (13:48). In Berea, the people receive the word with great eagerness (17:11), but opposition arises when Jews heard the word of God has been proclaimed in Berea as well (17:13).

All of Acts displays the word as entering contested spaces but conquering. Opposition occurs in every locale: Jerusalem, Judea, Samaria, and the ends of the earth. However, no matter what, the law of the Lord goes forth from Zion.

As Pao notes, one of the most striking factors is the absence of "word of God" references in the last eight chapters of Acts. "The word of God does not return to Jerusalem and Caesarea, places it had already conquered."[7] It comes and offers salvation, but once people have rejected it, it does not return again.

The word is thus personified as an active character in Acts.[8] This is because the Bible as a whole attributes to the word that which is attributed to God. For example, Isaiah 40:8 says the word of our God will stand forever. The word carries out God's will (Isa. 55:10–11).

Or as Joshua Jipp has put it, the word is a "travelling divine agent" or "visitation" people will either welcome or deny.[9] The word as an agent, a traveling force, likely hails from Isaiah 2:2–4:

> It shall come to pass in the latter days
>   that the mountain of the house of the LORD
> shall be established as the highest of the mountains,
>   and shall be lifted up above the hills;
> and all the nations shall flow to it,
>   and many peoples shall come, and say:
> "Come, let us go up to the mountain of the LORD,

---

7   Pao, *Acts and the Isaianic New Exodus*, 155.

8   The word in Acts has deeper Christology and creation theology ties than usually noted (John 1:1).

9   Joshua Jipp, *Divine Visitations and Hospitality to Strangers in Luke-Acts: An Interpretation of the Malta Episode in Acts 28:1–10* (Leiden: Brill, 2013), 236–40.

to the house of the God of Jacob,
that he may teach us his ways
    and that we may walk in his paths."
For out of Zion shall go forth the law,
    and the word of the Lord from Jerusalem.
He shall judge between the nations,
    and shall decide disputes for many peoples;
and they shall beat their swords into plowshares,
    and their spears into pruning hooks;
nation shall not lift up sword against nation,
    neither shall they learn war anymore.

Conclusion

The word spreads, grows, and multiplies in Acts. The main leaders in Jerusalem are opposed to its message. Cultural differences seek to distract from it. Satan tries to squash it. The kings of the earth try to halt it. Persecution and antagonism fill the narrative.

However, the word is a divine agent, and God cannot be held immobile or inert. If the Father is the author of the narrative, then he has many actors. Jesus is one of them. The Spirit is another. The word is also a divine actor. It takes on a life of its own in Acts, following the cues of earlier biblical authors.

The word progresses because the three persons of the Trinity are intimately related in the spread of the word. It goes forth according to the Father's plan, its content concerns Jesus, and its power stems from the Spirit. More specifically, the content of the word concerns the gospel about the King and his kingdom.

The emphasis in Acts on Jesus is on his risen and ascended status. This is not at the expense of the cross, but it does receive prominence. Jesus is the one who conquered death as the righteous one and has now been enthroned overall. This means the kingdom of God is present through the work of the King.

This message has power because it comes from the triune God, so it multiplies and conquers. It enters lands, defeats Satan, and offers forgiveness of sins. It has an energy of its own as the apostles go out with a message transcending their ability. Even when the apostles are suffering, in prison, or killed, the word spreads.

Every generation is tempted not only to abandon truth but also to make noncentral matters central. In Acts, the message is central. The gospel message is what is found on the apostles' lips. Luke does not conceive of a Christian who does not speak about the good news of Jesus. It is always their main subject and must be ours too.

Acts isn't so much about the apostles; it is about their message. The apostles all have died, but their word continues to grow and conquer—even today.

Salvation Spreads to All Flesh

*And there is salvation in no one else, for there
is no other name under heaven given among
men by which we must be saved.*

ACTS 4:12

Brothers and Sisters

A few chapters ago, I described a concert I attended in Portland. At
this same concert, I was introduced to another band, *The Brilliance*.
They are a liturgical band based out of New York who have a soft,
contemplative, and distressed sound. One of their most famous songs
is called "Brother." They write of how Christ's work compels us to be
reconciled to one another, even our enemies.

Luke hits on the same theme through the language "salvation to all
flesh." While we have a tendency to think of salvation in individualistic
terms, salvation in the Old Testament always includes a new community. Acts traces how God reconciles different cultures, ethnicities,
genders, and political enemies.

This book has focused on a logical and narratival order to the theological themes of Acts. A theology of Acts starts with the Father's plan,

the Son's rule, and the Spirit's empowering. This leads to the multiplying of God's word.

However, the word announces, enacts, and delivers salvation to all flesh. It reconciles and saves people in the name of Christ. Salvation to all flesh is a dominant theme in Acts. The vocabulary of salvation ("savior," "salvation," and "to save") proliferates especially in Luke-Acts.

No other writer uses *sōzein* and its cognate forms as much as Luke, and his second volume is no different. Luke employs the word twenty-one times, both in narrative and speech material. Joel Green even argues salvation is the theme of Acts that unifies other textual elements within the narrative.[1]

Luke doesn't put emphasis so much on what salvation is—that is assumed. Rather, Luke establishes who the Savior is, where salvation is to be found, and emphasizes the *presence* of salvation for all people by the Spirit. All of these realities cluster around Jesus, who bestows salvation (Acts 4:12; 5:31; 13:23; Luke 1:47, 69, 77; 2:11); the Spirit, who applies salvation (Acts 10:45–48; 11:14–15); and God, who plans salvation (Luke 3:4–6; Acts 28:25–28).

Our analysis will therefore look at the Jewish and Hellenistic background to salvation language, then at salvation as a theme in Acts, and finally at how salvation is offered to "all flesh" in Acts.

Table 5.1   Salvation to All Flesh

Background	A military term indicating rescue and relief from enemies but also the formation or protection of a community.
In Acts	Salvation is centered around the Davidic King who welcomes the marginalized and the "other."
To All Flesh	Salvation is status-inversion: it goes to Jerusalemites, Judeans, the Hellenized, Samaritans, God-fearers, pagans, and barbarians (in that order).

---

1   Joel B. Green, "Salvation to the Ends of the Earth: God as the Saviour in the Acts of the Apostles," in *Witness to the Gospel: The Theology of Acts*, ed. I. Howard Marshall and David Peterson (Grand Rapids, MI: Eerdmans, 1998), 83.

Salvation Background

In the Greek world, salvation means the bestowal of blessings and gifts.[2] One dictionary defines it as "to save, keep from harm, preserve, rescue, make well."[3] While the term is used comprehensively in the Scriptures of Christ's redemptive work, it is more precisely a military term.

If justification is a judicial metaphor, regeneration is material, reconciliation is social, adoption is familial, sanctification is cultic, and redemption is economic, then salvation is martial. This is supported in the Old Testament.

In the Old Testament, salvation denoted deliverance, preservation, and rescue (the term occurs frequently in Psalms, Isaiah, and Jeremiah). The term first appears when God rescues Israel from Egypt. Moses calls the people in Exodus 14:13 to stand firm and see the salvation God will accomplish for them. Yahweh then destroys Egypt in the sea and lets Israel walk on dry ground. In the song by the sea, the people sing, "The Lord is my strength and my song, / and he has become my salvation" (Ex. 15:2).

As readers continue through the Old Testament, "salvation" continues to communicate deliverance from enemies. When Israel enters the land, Moses tells the people they shall be saved from their enemies, referring primarily to the Canaanites (Num. 10:9). Moses also tells them the Lord will fight their battles and give them salvation (Deut. 20:4). Though the enemy has shifted from the Egyptians to the Canaanites, the idea is the same.

Later, while Israel's main opponent is the Philistines, Hannah prays, "My heart exults in the LORD; / my horn is exalted in the LORD. / My mouth derides my enemies, / because I rejoice in your salvation" (1 Sam. 2:1; see also Pss. 3:8; 18:2). Often, the psalmist cries out for God to save him (Pss. 12:1; 20:9; 28:9; 60:5). The prophets tell Israel to turn to God and be saved while in exile (Isa. 45:22; 59:1). So, salvation

---

2   W. Forester, "Sōzō, Sōtēria, Sōtēr, Sōtērios," in *TDNT* (Grand Rapids, MI: Eerdmans, 1971), 966–80.

3   NIDNTTE, ed. Moises Silva (Grand Rapids, MI: Zondervan, 2014), 4:420.

means safety from enemies, whether that be Egypt, the Canaanites, the Philistines, Assyria, or Babylon.[4]

However, in each of these instances, salvation was not only salvation *from* but salvation *to*. Israel was not only saved from Egypt but saved to a new covenant relationship with Yahweh. Israel needed to be saved from the Canaanites to continue their worship of Yahweh. Israel longed for salvation from Babylon so they could gather as a community again. Salvation and a new people group are intimately linked. This Old Testament background frames Luke's salvation terminology with imperial, political, and wartime imagery, all in order to form a new society.

Outside the Scriptures, this political yet communal reality is also supported in the wider culture. In the Hellenistic ruler cult, the term "Savior" became part of the official title of kings, and divine honors were accorded them. The phrase "savior god" was regularly incorporated into the Ptolemaic and Seleucid royal titles. Julius Caesar is described as the world's god, ruler, and savior.

Therefore, salvation in Old Testament and Greco-Roman times is a military idea centered on a ruler who comes and rescues his people by defeating their enemies so they can form a society in which their values and traditions are honored. Luke certainly intends this prevailing meaning with regard to Christ's salvation, but he also reconfigures it.

Salvation in Acts

The above analysis may wrongly suggest salvation in Acts is exclusively focused on a "this-worldly" reality. But even among pagans, the military victory of a nation was the victory of their gods. Luke follows this pattern and uses salvation to denote earthly realities, but these earthly realities have heavenly sources.

---

4   It is also clear it is the Lord who saves. Deuteronomy 33:29 says the people are saved by the Lord. Even when salvation seems to come from secondary causes, the Scriptures show the Lord saves. It is the Lord who raised up judges who saved Israel (Judg. 2:16, 18; 3:9, 31; 6:14–15). People are powerless to save (Jer. 14:9; Hos. 13:10). If they return to the Lord, they will be saved (Isa. 30:15).

Heaven and earth are not separate; they overlap. While readers should put "salvation" under the above imperial, political, and wartime banner, this should also be qualified and expanded by a few theological factors in Luke's writing.

First, Luke consistently ties salvation to "the forgiveness of sins" (Acts 2:38; 5:31; 10:43; 13:38; 15:9; 22:16; 26:18). Though the term primarily connoted physical deliverance in the Old Testament, the hope was connected with the people's rescue from sin (Isa. 43:25; 44:22; Jer. 31:34). Therefore, while it seldom expresses a spiritual state exclusively, the common sense was of physical deliverance accompanied with spiritual blessings. The two always intertwine in the Old Testament and in Acts. Luke subverts the common notion that our enemies are only outside of us. The enmity begins within. Our own fallenness is our fundamental problem.

Second, in Acts very little evidence subsists that Rome, Caesar, or the nations are the enemies. In fact, they are all invited into this salvation Jesus has accomplished. The enemies are sin, death, and the spiritual forces, which embody themselves in prideful and jealous leaders and corrupt all people from within.

But these leaders are found mainly in Jerusalem. Paul preaches Jesus as Savior, but Paul is also continually declared innocent in Acts by Rome. Luke narrates not just Paul's arrest by the rulers but also Paul's entrusting himself to Roman justice. Paul thrusts himself into the heart of the Empire so he can proclaim this salvation. John Barclay is surely right to say Paul does not "oppose Rome *as Rome*, but opposes anti-God powers wherever and however they manifest themselves on the human stage."[5]

In Acts, salvation is needed because of rebellion against Jesus (2:23; 3:13–15; 7:51–53), idolatry (17:29–31), and the future wrath of God (Luke 3:7, 9, 17). This applies to all people, both Jews and Gentiles. Salvation is therefore centered on the Davidic King, described as a gift of God, proclaimed to the nations, and results in incorporation into the people of God.

The anthropology and soteriology of Luke is not much different from that of the rest of the New Testament. People need salvation because they

---

5   John Barclay, *Pauline Churches and Diaspora Jews* (Grand Rapids, MI: Eerdmans, 2016), 387.

are sinners and under the power of the evil one. The enthroned Messiah is thus the benefactor of salvation, the one authorized to give this gift.

However, though interpreters should recognize this *spiritual* element, Luke does not wholly *spiritualize* it. Luke has a distinctly earthy and embodied view of salvation. The result of salvation in Luke's writings is reversal of social, spiritual, and physical status by "incorporation and participation in the Christocentric community of God's people."[6]

Salvation brought status-inversion, where the lowly and outcast are raised up and promised liberation.[7] This coheres with Jesus's paradigmatic and keynote speech in the Nazareth synagogue:

> The Spirit of the Lord is upon me, because he has anointed me to proclaim good news to the poor. He has sent me to proclaim liberty to the captives and recovering of sight to the blind, to set at liberty those who are oppressed, to proclaim the year of the Lord's favor. (Luke 4:18–19)

The centrality of Jesus being Savior and the status-inversion themes are seen clearly in the narrative pattern of Acts 2–3 and Acts 13–14. Peter and Paul preach Jesus as Savior in their two inaugural speeches, and then salvation actions follow. Salvation has come in word and deed.

In Peter's Pentecost speech, the enthronement of the Davidic King and the arrival of the Spirit compel Peter to quote from Joel 2:32, saying, "Everyone who calls upon the name of the Lord *shall be saved*" (Acts 2:21).

Built off this salvation preaching is the narrative embodiment of this theme in Acts 3–4. Though the term "save/salvation" is not used in Acts 3, Peter employs the term when he responds to the temple leaders' accusations, saying, "Are we being examined for *healing/saving* this man?" (4:9 my translation). Healing is salvation. They are the same Greek word.

---

6   Green, "Salvation to the Ends of the Earth," 91.

7   Bock says, "Salvation in Luke is a broad concept. It is about comprehensive deliverance and restoration. It is pictured in the signs of the scope of Jesus' healings as well as those of the apostles. It frees people from sin, from Satan, and from darkness, it results in forgiveness, the gift of the Spirit, and incorporation into the people of God made up of all nations." Darrell L. Bock, *A Theology of Luke and Acts: God's Promised Program, Realized for All Nations*, ed. Andreas J. Köstenberger (Grand Rapids, MI: Zondervan, 2012), 237.

The healing of the crippled man was not merely a medical restoration but a comprehensive, multidimensional salvation. Peter preaches salvation at Pentecost and then spreads salvation to the lame man.

Paul's paradigmatic presentation follows the same pattern: salvation in word and deed. In Pisidian Antioch, the predominant focus is on his message of King and Savior Jesus. The concepts "savior" and "salvation" get particular focus (13:23, 26, 47)—presenting this as a message about a superior Savior. Some of the Jews reject Paul's message, so he says he and his companions have been sent to the Gentiles. He then quotes from Isaiah 49:6 and links his mission back to Acts 1:8:

> "'I have made you a light for the Gentiles,
>   that you may bring salvation to the ends of the earth.'" (Acts 13:47)

Then, mirroring Peter's salvation sermon and deed in Acts 2–4, Paul goes to Lystra and heals a lame man (14:8–10). This again is not merely a physical healing but a multidimentional salvation. Bede says, "Just as that lame man whom Peter and John cured at the door of the temple prefigured salvation for the Jews, so too this sick Lycaonian prefigured the people of the Gentiles."[8]

Though interpreters might be tempted to spiritualize much of Luke's language, what is really taking place is a reconfiguration of salvation that includes both heavenly and earthly realities.

To All Flesh

We have seen how salvation is a multidimensional reality in the name of Jesus. One other point is necessary to cover here. In Acts, this salvation is not exclusive but inclusive. It is proclaimed to the nations (1:8; 8:4–40; 9:15; 10:34–43; 13:46–48; 22:21; 28:25–28). The rescue is for all peoples. Acts has a universal focus (10:34–36, 42–43; 15:7–11; 26:17–18, 22–23).

---

8   Francis Martin, ed., *Acts*, Ancient Christian Commentary Series (Downers Grove, IL: InterVarsity Press, 2006), 175. Venerable Bede, *The Venerable Bede Commentary on the Acts of the Apostles*, trans. Lawrence T. Martin (Kalamazoo, MI: Cistercian Publications, 1989), 14.8 (125).

This emphasis can be seen in the phrase "salvation of God," which bookends Luke's two-volume narrative pointing to Gentile inclusion. First, John the Baptist quotes Isaiah 40:3–5 in Luke 3:4–6, stating, "*all flesh* shall see the *salvation* of God." Interestingly, no other Gospel writer includes this phrase when they quote from Isaiah 40 at the beginning of their work.

Second, at the end of Acts, Paul quotes Isaiah 6:9–10 in 28:25–28, stating "let it be known to you that this *salvation* of God has been sent *to the Gentiles*; they will listen." John the Baptist announces the universal welcome before Jesus. Paul announces it after Jesus.

Table 5.2   Salvation to All Flesh in Luke and Acts

Luke 3:4–6 quoting Isaiah 40:3–5	Acts 28:25–28 quoting Isaiah 6:9–10
As it is written in the book of the words Isaiah the prophet: "The voice of one crying out in the wilderness: 'Prepare the way of the Lord; make his paths straight. Every valley shall be filled, and every mountain and hill shall be made low; and the crooked shall become straight, and the rough places shall become level ways, *and all flesh shall see the salvation of God.*"	"The Holy Spirit was right in saying to your fathers through Isaiah the prophet: "Go to this people, and say, You will indeed hear but never understand, and you will indeed see but never perceive. For this people's heart has grown dull, and with their ears they can barely hear, and their eyes they have closed; lest they should see with their eyes and hear with their ears and understand with their heart and turn, and I would heal them. Therefore let it be known to you that *this salvation of God has been sent to the Gentiles*; they will listen."

Both of these texts hail from Isaiah, indicating the gathering of Gentiles has been part of the plan all along. Abraham was promised he would be the father of many nations, and Isaiah said everyone will see the salvation of God and salvation will be sent to the Gentiles. Therefore, in Acts, the spread of the salvation message to all flesh is not so much new as it is the fulfillment of God's original plan.

In Acts, Luke traces this theme in concentric circles. He moves from those most expected to receive salvation to the least expected.[9] If Jerusalem and Judea are put at the center, then each circle represents further prejudice that coheres with the narrative flow of Acts.

Figure 5.1   Salvation to All Flesh

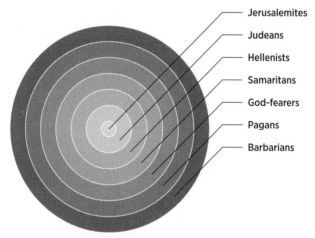

Jerusalemites

Judeans

Hellenists

Samaritans

God-fearers

Pagans

Barbarians

Initially, those most expected are offered salvation (Jerusalem), but as Acts keeps progressing, salvation moves all the way to barbarians and to Rome itself (Acts 27–28). Luke moves from Jerusalemites, to Judeans, to Hellenists, to Samaritans, to God-fearers, to Gentiles who have never worshiped Yahweh, and finally to barbarians. Too many are content with lumping all the Gentiles together. However, it is better

---

9   Justo L. Gonzalez, *The Story Luke Tells: Luke's Unique Witness to the Gospel* (Grand Rapids, MI: Eerdmans, 2015), 39–40.

to speak of Gentiles not as a monolithic category but a diverse reality. There are *Gentiles*, not a Gentile.

A specific ripple effect resides in Acts. Though I won't trace them all out, three key examples of diverse Gentiles and the offer of salvation are highlighted below: the God-fearer Cornelius (Acts 10–11), Roman officers and pagan seamen (Acts 27), and the barbarians on Malta (Acts 28).

The Cornelius episode is a key juncture in Acts. While many people view it this way, we need to be precise about *who* Cornelius is and *what* happens. First, Cornelius is not the run-of-the-mill Gentile. Though he is a centurion, living in Caesarea, he is also a God-fearer like the eunuch (8:27; 10:2). Cornelius had knowledge of God's salvation, but it was incomplete without hearing of Christ's glorification. This devotion to Yahweh evidenced itself in *many charitable deeds* for Jews and prayer (10:2).

Second, the Cornelius episode is important because not merely one Gentile is welcomed (like the eunuch) but a whole Gentile household. Peter, in his defense to Jerusalem, upholds the reality that Cornelius *and his household* are baptized (11:14). This phrase, *him and his household*, is important. Cornelius and a group of Gentiles are saved.

When Peter goes to visit him, he found "many persons" gathered there (10:27). When Peter arrives, Cornelius says, "*We* are all here in the presence of God" (10:33). Peter preaches that "in *every* nation *anyone* who fears him and does what is right is acceptable to him" (10:35). While Peter was saying these things about Jesus, the Holy Spirit "fell *on all* who heard the word" (10:44).

As readers already know, the gift of the Spirit is the gift of salvation. Yet, the communal nature of this gift, which is often passed over quickly, is key to the narrative. *Gentiles*, not merely a Gentile, have been welcomed. Plural subjects and objects dominate the narrative, indicating the shift is more corporate than that in the eunuch episode, as a new household is brought into a new community.

The progression of salvation to all flesh is also evident in the last two chapters of Acts. Acts 27 has confused interpreters about its placement in the narrative. Why would Luke spend so much time on the storm and shipwreck at sea?

But if one of Luke's primary purposes is to describe how God's salvation has been granted to *both* Jews and Gentiles, then this first part of the journey details Paul's witnessing and offering salvation to seafaring Gentiles and Roman officers.

Luke makes sure to mention the centurion of the Augustan Cohort multiple times (27:1, 3, 6, 11, 31, 43) and even by name (Julius) a few times (27:1, 3). The pilot and owner of the ship (27:11), the sailors (27:27, 30–32, 42), and even the number of persons on the ship (27:37) are also mentioned.

Acts 27 is thus the final "missionary journey to the Gentiles." Paul comes to the Greeks, enters their worldview, and shows how Yahweh is greater than all their gods. The spread of salvation to pagan seamen and a Roman officer is seen in two ways: (1) Paul's prophetic portrait, where he bestows "salvation," and (2) the Greek sea imagery.

Paul acts as a prophet who leads those on the boat to salvation. Though the courtroom scenes in Acts depict Paul as prophet, he is seen mainly on the defensive. Here, Paul prophecies, provides food, becomes the source of salvation for those on the boat, and receives visions of encouragement along his way. As prophet, he leads them through the sea and to the promised land. As on his other "missionary journeys," Paul does not undertake this task alone. He is joined by Aristarchus and the "we" party along the way (27:1–8, 18–20, 37; 28:1–2, 7, 10).

As they journey, the storm at sea threatens destruction to all on the boat. In the Hebrew Bible, plunging into the waters was symbolic of going to one's death. Being saved out of them is resurrection.[10] Six

---

10 Brandon D. Crowe, *The Hope of Israel: The Resurrection of Christ in the Acts of the Apostles* (Grand Rapids, MI: Baker Academic, 2020), 83. Goulder says the whole of Acts 27 is devoted to the account of the shipwreck and so the incident occupies a central position symbolically in the whole book. It therefore makes sense to view it as a death-resurrection-ascension story since this is one of the primary themes of Luke. This also fits because the previous section was Paul's trial, then he enters death, and is raised unto life in order to save many. Goulder goes on to say, "The theme of Christ's death and resurrection thus

times in the narrative, the term "salvation" is employed but is usually translated as "safety" or "safely" (27:20, 31, 34, 43, 44; 28:1, 4). Luke wants to highlight that all on the boat reach safety (i.e., salvation).

Though many commentators view this as purely "physical" salvation, it more likely hints at something more. As already demonstrated with the lame men in Jerusalem and Lystra, Luke's pattern is to display physical and spiritual salvation as united. Paul acts as the prophet who leads them to salvation.

This prophetic portrait and the Gentile focus is further supported by Old Testament echoes. Paul becomes a new Jonah, but unlike Jonah, he does not run from the will of God but follows God's plan to a foreign nation to preach the good news. The parallels between the story of Jonah and Paul are abundant, even though Jonah is a negative example, while Paul is a positive one:

1. Jonah sails to escape God's call; Paul's sails to fulfill God's will.
2. Both Jonah and Paul head westward and encounter fierce storms.
3. In both stories, God uses the wind and waves to show his sovereignty.
4. Both Paul's and Jonah's vocations are clarified.
5. Jonah's presence was the cause of the storm, while Paul's presence was the reason for deliverance from the storm.

Luke's focus on salvation to Gentiles in Acts 27 is also evident in Paul's final journey by the emphasis on the setting. The minutiae of the storm, ship, sea, and shipwreck are immediately noticeable to any reader. Since the sea was largely a Greek place, Paul becomes a seafaring prophet who can direct pagans in their own spaces. Jews were more land-bound, and the sea represented the chaotic.

The sea was not merely the Greek sea but the place of demonic chaos that only Yahweh could subdue (Ex. 15:1–8; Isa. 51:9–10). This journey

---

dominates the climax of all nine cycles but the first: gradually in the apostles' persecutions, openly in Stephen's and Peter's, indirectly in the first three Pauline journeys, triumphantly in his progress to Rome." M. D. Goulder, *Type and History in Acts* (London: SPCK, 1964), 50; cf. 39.

is ethnic, political, and cosmic. These realities are intertwined. This is confirmed in Jewish literature. Though God is portrayed as sovereign over the sea, the sea births evil:

- Isaiah 17:12–13 describes the raging of nations like the raging of the sea.
- Isaiah 27:1 speaks of the Lord slaying the monster of the sea, Leviathan, that coiling serpent.
- In Daniel 7:3, the four beasts representing Empires came out from the sea.
- Habakkuk 3:8–15 says Yahweh trampled the sea by his horses.

Connecting Paul's voyage to this worldview indicates that Paul's message conquers not only the Behemoth of the land but also the Leviathan of the sea. God controls the winds and uses them to accomplish his purposes. Paul and his shipmates move from darkness to light as God directs them through the storm and into places where Paul can spread the salvation of Jesus.

If in Athens Paul beats the philosophers at their own game, and in Ephesus he shows the power of his "magic," then this scene represents a parallel act of narrative aggression.[11] Salvation is offered to all flesh, even those on the sea and Roman officers.

The final example of salvation to all flesh is the Malta episode (Acts 28:1–10). Here, Luke shows how *barbarians* (the ESV labels them "native people") are presented with salvation. After Paul's shipwreck, the group didn't know who would greet them. In that time, it was a common trope to worry about who would meet you after a shipwreck. Odysseus lamented landing on unknown islands, fearing for his safety.

"Barbarians" in the modern sense has a pejorative meaning but simply refers to non-Greeks here. No brothers and sisters wait for Paul and his companions (cf. 21:7–17), no friends (cf. 27:3), and no synagogue. It is a group of barbarians who welcome Paul and his shipmates.

---

11 Loveday Alexander, *Acts in Its Ancient Literary Context: A Classicist Looks at the Acts of the Apostles*, LNTS 298 (New York: Bloomsbury T&T Clark, 2005), 84.

However, this does not take away from the surprise in the narrative. Barbarians fulfill Greco-Roman virtue expectations more than the elite in Philippi, the philosophers in Athens, the powerful in Ephesus, and the sacred in Jerusalem.[12] The local people surprisingly show "hospitality" and light a fire as it was cold and raining.[13]

Luke subverts the cultural stereotype of these people by showing they embody high Hellenistic expectations and are characterized in the same line as the Good Samaritan, Mary, Zacchaeus, Cornelius, and Lydia. Salvation goes to all flesh.

As Jipp has shown, the Malta episode operates according to the logic of a theoxeny.[14] A theoxeny is an account in Greek mythology where someone shows unknowing hospitality to a god—or in this case, the emissary of God. The following components typically characterize these types of scenes that align with Paul's visit to Malta.

Table 5.3   Paul's Visit on Malta as a Theoxeny

Components of a Theoxeny	Theoxeny in the Malta Episode
Hospitality or inhospitality shown to an unknown host who is actually a divine guest.	The barbarians show hospitality to Paul even though he is a total stranger to them.
Recognition scene where the divine identity of the stranger is revealed.	Once Paul does not die by the snake bite, his identity as one who embodies the power of Jesus is revealed.
Rewards or retribution for the host based on their response is given.	Paul bestows gifts on the Maltese, further showing his power over death.

12 Craig S. Keener, *Acts: An Exegetical Commentary*, vol. 4, *24:1–28:31* (Grand Rapids, MI: Baker Academic, 2012), 3664.

13 Greeks often criticized barbarians for their lack of "hospitality," which Greeks prized. For example, Odysseus, when he encounters a new land, says, "Alas, to the land of what mortals have I now come? Are they insolent, wild, and unjust? Or are they hospitable to strangers and fear the gods in their thoughts?" (Homer, *Odyssey* 6.119–121). But not all barbarians are criticized in these ways. See Joshua Jipp, *Divine Visitations and Hospitality to Strangers in Luke-Acts: An Interpretation of the Malta Episode in Acts 28:1–10* (Leiden: Brill, 2013), 41, 257.

14 Jipp, *Divine Visitations*; Joshua Jipp, *Reading Acts*, Cascade Companions (Eugene, OR: Cascade Books, 2018), 127–30.

The point is not that Paul is divine, but rather that he carries the divine presence with him by the Spirit. Those on Malta claim he is a god! Their hospitality, which bookends the narrative, symbolically shows the acceptance of this message. Paul tramples on snakes and spreads the news of Jesus's salvation.

The Malta episode becomes a final and climactic episode of divine visitation in Gentile territory.[15] Rome is next. Salvation to all flesh has moved from Jerusalem to Hellenists, to Samaritans, to a eunuch, to Cornelius's household (a God-fearer), to a larger group of Gentiles in Antioch, to a Gentile mission, to seafaring Greeks and a Roman centurion, and finally to barbarians. Salvation in Jesus's name is for all humanity.

Conclusion

God's plan all along was to form a people. In Acts, the apostles proclaim salvation to all flesh in the name of Jesus. The word goes forth as Isaiah predicted, creating brothers and sisters out of enemies. God's plan is coming to fulfillment not only in Jesus, but in the church—Jesus's body.

Salvation was primarily a military term, but people in the Ancient Near East didn't have as strong a distinction between spiritual and physical rescue. In the Old Testament, Yahweh saved Israel from their enemies: Egypt, Canaanites, Philistines, Assyria, and Babylon.

However, the Old Testament also promised that Abraham would one day have an innumerable family. Isaiah said all nations would see the salvation of God. Salvation results in social, spiritual, and physical reversal. People are saved and incorporated into a new community.

Luke picks up this thread and employs salvation terminology to a greater extent than any other New Testament author. Salvation is rescue and relief. Salvation is status-inversion. It is centered on Jesus the Messiah, applied by the Spirit, and according to God's plan.

15 Jipp, *Reading Acts*, 129; Ronald H. Van der Bergh, "The Missionary Character of Paul's Stay on Malta (Acts 28:1–10) According to the Early Church," *JECH* 3, no.1 (2013): 83–97. Van der Bergh shows how in the history of interpretation, this episode was viewed as a missionary action of Paul. However, Chrysostom takes their statement of Paul as a god as an excess like that at Lystra. Chrysostom, Homily 54 on Acts, in *NPNF*, Series 1, vol. 11, ed. Philip Schaff (Grand Rapids, MI: Eerdmans, 1925), 320.

Luke's specific contribution to the biblical discussion of salvation is threefold. First, he shows in Acts that salvation is found in Jesus, the Davidic King. Second, he identifies the main antagonists as sin, death, and Satan. Finally, he shows how salvation is a status-inversion. It goes to all flesh: Jerusalemites, Judeans, the Hellenized, Samaritans, God-fearers, women, and pagans all are offered salvation.

Though we might be tempted to think the main problem with the world is other Christians who hold positions different from our own, or the other political party, or the other race, or the other gender, Luke reminds us that our main enemies stem from within (our sin) and without (Satan), which produce chaos (death).

This is not to deny the social reality of sin, but to remember the emphasis in the Scriptures is upon our own need for a Savior. We need salvation from ourselves and from evil spiritual forces. And according to Luke, this salvation is offered to everyone. It doesn't matter their skin color, socioeconomic background, or social status.

God's plan is to make enemies brothers and sisters, to reconcile those who would never have been in the same room together. While those in Luke's day may have been wondering whether the plan of the church was on track, his narrative shows salvation is on its way to every corner of the world. Those in Jerusalem, in Asia Minor, in Macedonia and Achaia, in Ephesus, and those on the sea, on the land, and in Rome will hear of this salvation.

The Church Is Established

So the church throughout all Judea and Galilee and Samaria
had peace and was being built up. And walking in the fear of
the Lord and in the comfort of the Holy Spirit, it multiplied.

ACTS 9:31

The People of God

The Father's plan was to create a diverse community of people who follow his Son by the power of the Spirit. In Acts, Luke shows God's new people are established. God builds his church by the power of the Spirit, and the church witnesses to others about the presence of resurrection life.

However, readers of Acts must again be precise. Though some think Acts is the story of the church, it begins with the triune God and his rescue in Christ. The church is built upon God and his word, the message of salvation. Yet this does not mean the apostles or the community of Jesus are sidelined. They merely come logically after, since God is the *primum movens* (first mover).

However, God's primacy does not diminish the agency or the importance of the church. God acts in and through his image bearers (by the Spirit and through his word) to overhaul the space of the earth. Those who turn to Christ are formed by the power of the Spirit to become the new Israel, temple, and people of God.

Though this chapter could look at the church in Acts from a variety of angles, I will follow the larger narrative sequence for the people of God in Acts. Luke presents three panels for the progression and complexion of the church: restoring Israel, assembling outcasts, and welcoming Gentiles.[1]

Jerusalem is first. God comes to Israel first in order that they might bless the nations. Then the word spreads to outcasts (Samaritans, a eunuch, an enemy of the church, and a Gentile household). Finally, the Gentile mission commences. God establishes a new assembly comprised of various people groups.

Table 6.1   God's People in Acts

Acts 1–7	Restoring Israel
Acts 8–12	Assembling Outcasts
Acts 13–28	Welcoming Gentiles

Restoring Israel (1–7)

The first stage of God's people is Israel's restoration.[2] The first seven chapters of Acts focus on Jerusalem and the temple. As James Dunn states, "It began in Jerusalem. That is the first clear message which Luke wants his readers to understand."[3] God's temple blessings flow *from* and *through* Israel. The first section (Acts 1–7) thus demarcates

---

1   This outline largely follows David Seccombe, "The New People of God," in *Witness to the Gospel: The Theology of Acts*, ed. I. Howard Marshall and David Peterson (Grand Rapids, MI: Eerdmans, 1998), 349–72. Both Peter and Paul, the two main figures in Acts, portray this growth in temple terms in their letters (1 Pet. 2:5–6; 1 Cor. 3:9–17; Eph. 2:19–22).

2   Luke does not use the term *ekklēsia* until Acts 5:11 in the Ananias and Sapphira episode, but he employs it eighteen times after that (8:1, 3; 9:31; 11:22, 26; 12:1, 5; 13:1; 14:23, 27; 15:3–4, 22, 41; 16:5; 18:22; 20:17, 28). It may seem odd that Luke does not use the term in the first four chapters, but the concept is present, and he does employ the circumlocution for the assembly *epi to auto* ("upon the same," translated sometimes as "together" or "assemble") in 1:15; 2:1, 44, 47; 4:26.

3   James D. G. Dunn, *The Acts of the Apostles* (Grand Rapids, MI: Eerdmans, 1996), 1.

the remnant of Israel. Some respond positively, but others, especially the temple leaders, reject this life and continue to cling to the old temple.

Acts begins with Jesus commanding his disciples to wait for the promised Spirit. This is a key promise that inaugurates Israel's renewal (Jer. 31:31–34; Ezek. 36:26–27). Israel's restoration is further indicated in the choosing of Matthias as the twelfth apostle (Acts 1:15–26). Though many struggle to know what to do with the placement of this narrative, at least one of Luke's points is the choice of the twelfth disciple makes symbolic Israel whole again (Luke 22:30; Acts 26:7).

God has promised "to raise up the tribes of Jacob / and to bring back the preserved of Israel" (Isa. 49:6) and "Ephraim's envy will cease; Judah's harassing will end" (Isa. 11:13 CSB). Now Israel's reconstitution is partially fulfilled as the twelfth disciple is chosen, thus reuniting the tribes separated after the time of Solomon.

Pentecost also restores Israel by gathering in exiles scattered abroad. Pentecost was a pilgrimage festival in which Jews from all nations would gather into their city. The Spirit falls at Pentecost because God had regathered Israel (Isa. 44:1–4). God had promised he would bring his offspring from the east, west, north, and south (Isa. 43:5–7; Acts 2:9–11).

Therefore, the Spirit comes at Pentecost to reconstitute the gathered people of God. Not only have the twelve tribes been symbolically reunited, but also the exiles of Israel scattered during the reign of Assyria, Babylon, Persia, Greece, and Rome are regathered.

Pentecost also symbolizes the establishment of the new temple because those gathered receive the presence of God. In Ezekiel, God's Spirit departed from the temple, and in Ezra, it did not return. Now the Spirit descends again. The new era is here (Luke 3:16–17; Acts 2:22–36).

The remaking of Israel continues as Peter's Pentecost sermon is directed to Jews. He speaks to them as Jewish men (Acts 2:14), Israelites (2:22), and "all the house of Israel" (2:36). In Ezekiel 37, "all the house of Israel" is associated with the regathering of Israel's exiles (37:21), the restoration of the north and south (37:15–22), the resurrection of Israel (37:15–22), the reign of the Davidic King (37:24–25), and the dwelling of God with his people (37:26–28). Acts 2 as a whole condenses restoration images found in Ezekiel.[4]

Table 6.2   Ezekiel in Acts 2

Acts 2	Ezekiel
2:5–11 Israelites gather from the entire diaspora	37:15–22 Reunification of the divided tribes of Israel in the land
2:4 They were all filled with the Holy Spirit	37:14 The pouring out of God's Spirit on his people
2:36 "Let all the house of Israel therefore know"	20:40; 36:10; 37:11 "The whole house of Israel" = the twelve tribes
2:29–36 The risen Jesus is the royal descendant of David	37:24–25 A new David = messianic King

Further supporting the establishment of God's people at Pentecost is the content of Peter's sermon (2:14–41). It becomes a textbook example of how God has fulfilled his promises to Israel in the resurrection and ascension of Jesus and the gift of the Spirit. All the passages Peter cites explain that this is part of God's plan: God promised the Spirit (Joel 2:28–32), the resurrection (Ps. 16:8–11), and the ascension (Ps. 110:1). Peter then tells Israel they must repent and be baptized in the name of Jesus (Acts 2:38) to be renewed. This message of repentance reiterates the prophets' message to Israel (Jer. 4:28; Joel 2:12–14). The new people of God are defined around the ascended Christ. They are to show their participation in the new community by going through water like the Israel of old.

The rest of Acts 3–7 can also be read through the lens of Israel's restoration. This is indicated by the temple focus until the end of chap-

---

4   This chart is adapted from notes Tim Mackie sent me in a personal email.

ter 7. An *inclusio* links Acts 2:46 and 5:42, which places the intervening narrative under the banner of "temple actions:"

> And day by day, attending the temple together and breaking bread in their homes, they received their food with glad and generous hearts. (2:46)

> And every day, in the temple and from house to house, they did not cease teaching and preaching that the Christ is Jesus. (5:42)

Between these texts are two temple restoration and conflict narratives, two interludes defining the people of God, and finally the section ends with Stephen's climactic temple sermon. It can be viewed visually like this:

Table 6.3   Temple Stories in Acts 3–7

1.	Temple Restoration and Conflict (3:1–4:31)	Peter heals and is arrested
A.	Defining the True People of God (4:32–5:11)	Barnabas gives, Ananias and Sapphira lie
2.	Temple Restoration and Conflict (5:12–42)	Healings and arrest
A.	Defining the True People of God (6:1–7)	Hellenistic widows are cared for
3.	Temple Sermon (6:8–8:3)	Stephen proclaims God's transcendent presence

In the first temple restoration and conflict story, Peter heals a lame man who sits outside the temple (3:2–3) and who is then welcomed into the temple once he is made whole (3:8). The priests and captain of the temple oppose them (4:1), Peter preaches Jesus as the rejected stone (4:11), and then God shakes the earth again like at Sinai when his people pray (4:31). The narrative is filled with temple themes. A new temple community has arrived with Jesus as the cornerstone.

A small narrative in Acts 4:32–5:11 further defines Israel, building on the summary in 2:44–47. Barnabas's generosity in the new community is contrasted to Ananias and Sapphira. The temple was more than a religious center, being also a social, political, and *economic* center from which the blessings of God flowed to the world. Barnabas's gift is highlighted. He is a Levite from Cyprus. Levites were set apart to perform priestly duties (Num. 1:47–53), following the golden calf incident (Ex. 32:26–29). A new Levite joins the community in contrast to the priestly rulers who oppose Peter and John (Acts 4:1).

However, Luke juxtaposes Barnabas's generosity with Ananias and Sapphira, who lie about their gift. The Old Testament echoes point to their action being not merely an arbitrary sin but an improper temple offering in contrast to the Levite's gift.[5] Jeremiah condemned the temple for becoming a den of robbers, and God's judgment is banishment from his presence (Jer. 7:11, 15). Ananias and Sapphira's dead bodies are removed, keeping the holy space pure just as when Achan was removed in the wilderness (Josh. 7). The boundaries of the new congregation of God are defined.

The second temple narrative is similar to the first, but this time the focus is on opposition (Acts 5:12–42). Yet God redeems the new congregation from their troubles, and Gamaliel notes that if these men are doing God's work, it will not be stopped. A second transition occurs with the selection of the seven to serve Hellenistic widows (6:1–7). Now the concern fans out, not away from Israel, but to those who are influenced by Greek culture. Their Greek inculturation caused them to be objects of scorn.

In this story, the barriers between Hellenized and Hebraic Jews are overcome as seven Hellenistic leaders are chosen to care for Hellenistic widows. As the community expands, God directs its generosity

---

5   Le Donne rightly argues that in Acts 1–7 the Holy Spirit restores the temple presence of the Lord and that this narrative should be viewed in that light, even though the specific location of Solomon's Portico is not explicit in this section as it is in 3:11 and 5:12. Anthony Le Donne, "The Improper Temple Offering of Ananias and Sapphira," *NTS* 59, no. 3 (2013): 346–64.

to all who enter and also introduces the Hellenized leaders, Stephen and Philip.

The Jerusalem narrative cycle comes to a climax at Stephen's trial, speech, and death (6:8–8:3). Opposition has been escalating, and now a Hellenized witness is martyred. Stephen is accused of disrespecting the temple and law. He responds with a salvation historical argument about the temporary and corrupt nature of the physical temple and the reception of God's prophets through history.

Stephen shows God's transcendent presence will not be limited by any building, region, or even people group; it is found only in the person of Jesus. God appeared to Abraham in a foreign land (7:2). He was with Joseph and Moses in Egypt (7:9, 20). God appeared to Moses in the burning bush in Midian (7:30–33). God appeared to Moses at Mount Sinai (7:38). These were all outside the land and before the temple. Stephen refutes the physical temple as a necessity for God's presence, though it functioned as a blessing in its time. God is not and cannot be localized and he spreads his temple presence to all who repent and believe.

Acts 1–7 is about the renewal of Israel. It concerns God's temple people and the invitation for Israel to be restored to God through faith in the Messiah. Many welcome this message and are engrafted into the community, but others reject it. The good news of Jesus Christ is proclaimed to both the Hebraic and Hellenized Jews in Jerusalem. Now expansion of God's people begins as Stephen's blood colors the earth.

Assembling Outcasts (8–12)

In Acts 8–12, the message spreads to outcasts. God assembles people on the margins of Israel. The glory of the temple will no longer be restricted to Jerusalem. Rivers of living water flow to the outer courts, breaking down walls and bringing life. Not only will the new community be restored to its previous state, but new members are received into it as well.

This assembling of outcasts fulfills promises of the Old Testament. In Isaiah 56:8, the prophet writes, "The Lord GOD, who gathers the outcasts of Israel, declares, '*I will gather yet others to him besides those already gathered.*'" He tells them to "let the outcasts of Moab sojourn among you" (Isa. 16:4). A variety of vignettes occur in Acts 8–12:

Table 6.4   Assembling Outcasts in Acts 8–12

Agent	Recipient	Symbol
Philip	Samaria	Northern Israel
Philip	Eunuch	Ethnic and Sexual
Jesus	Saul	Enemy of the Church
Peter	Cornelius and Household	God-fearer/Gentile

The Philip narrative has two parts, both dealing with those on the outskirts of Judaism: Samaritans and an Ethiopian eunuch. Both are outcasts and have an uncomfortable relationship with the temple. Samaritans rejected the Jerusalem temple, and eunuchs could not even pass through the court of the Gentiles. But God refused to be bound by temple obstacles.

Samaria was separated socially, geographically, and even religiously from their Jerusalem kin.[6] Most importantly, they worshiped on a different mountain: Mount Gerizim. The background to the relationship between Jews and Samaritans goes back to 1 Kings 12 and the rebellion of the northern kingdom against the southern kingdom. Samaritans were thus viewed as descendants of Jeroboam's rebellion against the house of David (1 Kings 12:16–20).

6   Omri, of the northern kingdom, ended up building the city of Samaria (1 Kings 16:24), and it became the capital of the northern kingdom, as Jerusalem was the capital of the southern kingdom. Both the north and the south were exiled, but those who remained in the land intermarried with Canaanites. When the exiles came back, they sought permission from Alexander the Great to build a temple on Mount Gerizim, and they had their own form of the Pentateuch. The Samaritans, therefore, had a different capital, different customs, and a different temple. Bock notes how they were treated as half-breeds: to eat with a Samaritan was said to be like eating pork, their daughters were seen as unclean, and they were accused of aborting fetuses. Darrell L. Bock, *Acts*, BECNT (Grand Rapids, MI: Baker Academic, 2007), 324.

However, Samaria receives the word with much joy (Acts 8:8). Philip's mission overcomes nationalistic borders and ethnic prejudices. Before the Gentile outreach can commence, Israel's north and south must be reintegrated. The hope of the prophets was that all Israel would be reassembled through the power of God's Spirit. Ezekiel speaks of a time when the stick of Judah (the South) and stick of Ephraim (the North) will be joined together (Ezek. 37:16–17). Yahweh will

> make them one nation in the land. . . . And one king shall be king over them all, and they shall be no longer two nations, and no longer divided into two kingdoms. They shall not defile themselves anymore with their idols and their detestable things, or with any of their transgressions. But I will save . . . and will cleanse them; and they shall be my people, and I will be their God.
>
> My servant David shall be king over them, and they shall all have one shepherd. (Ezek. 37:22–24)

This welcoming of the Samaritans into the new community is confirmed by the strange account of the delayed reception of the Spirit (Acts 8:14–17). The Jerusalem apostles must come pray and lay hands on them before they receive the Spirit. The "delay" of the Spirit can be confusing. To some, it looks like those in Samaria were saved and then received the Spirit, indicating a second blessing, or a two-stage experience of faith—water baptism and then Holy Spirit baptism.

However, this more likely is an exceptional circumstance recounted because of the rift between Jerusalem and Samaria. Samaria must wait for the Spirit, and Jerusalem must witness it. The outcome, therefore, is twofold—affecting both the Samaritans and the apostles. The Jerusalem apostles are convinced of God's love for the Samaritans as they witness the pouring out of the Spirit, which is a mark of the new age (Acts 2; 8; 10; cf. Luke 3:16). The Samaritans see they are connected to and not separate from the Jerusalem church.

Philip then goes south to a eunuch at the energizing direction of the Spirit. As Mikael Parson's asserts, with this episode, Luke radically redraws the map of who is in and who is out under Scriptural warrant.[7] Though Luke describes this character in great detail, the label "eunuch" sticks out, pointing primarily to gender and ethnic inclusion themes.

Being a eunuch means he was emasculated. Eunuchs were both prized and demonized: demonized because of their sexual ambiguity and prized because of their trustworthiness. They were considered effeminate or "non-men" sitting between the male-female binary. Philo writes that eunuchs are "neither male nor female."[8] Yet it is significant that the eunuch in Acts 8 is still described as a man. He is also an Ethiopian—a black man. Ethiopia was a remote land according to the Scriptures (Est. 1:1; 8:9; Ezek. 29:10), and Ethiopians were dark-complexioned people (Jer. 13:23), often used as a standard against which antiquity measured other people of color. The Ethiopian embodied the distant south.

In the Jewish Scriptures, eunuchs are ritually unclean and kept out of the temple (Lev. 21:20; 22:24; Deut. 23:1). However, Philip explains Jesus to him and baptizes him on the desert road. As the eunuch reads Isaiah 53, Isaiah 56 is fulfilled—which is only a few inches down on the Isaiah scroll:

> Let not the foreigner who has joined himself to the LORD say,
>   "The LORD will surely separate me from his people";
> and let not the eunuch say,
>   "Behold, I am a dry tree."
> For thus says the LORD:
> "To the eunuchs who keep my Sabbaths,
>   who choose the things that please me
>   and hold fast my covenant,
> I will give in my house and within my walls
>   a monument and a name

---

7   Mikeal C. Parsons, *Acts*, Paideia (Grand Rapids, MI: Baker Academic, 2008), 124.

8   *The Works of Philo Judaeus*, trans. C. D. Yonge (London: H. G. Bohn, 1854), 376; (Philo, *Somn.* 2.184). Cf. Brittany E. Wilson, "'Neither Male nor Female': The Ethiopian Eunuch in Acts 8.26–40," *NTS* 60, no. 3 (2014): 403–22.

better than sons and daughters;
   I will give them an everlasting name
      that shall not be cut off. (Isa. 56:3–5)

The third narrative of an outcast welcomed is Saul. An adversary of the church is changed by a vision of Jesus. The great enemy of the church is installed as the great missionary of the church.

Throughout this text, the central imagery concerns light and darkness. After Saul sees the light of Jesus, he is commissioned to bring this light to the Gentiles. Jesus's blinding appearance to Saul reminds readers of Ezekiel's vision when the heavens were opened and he saw brilliant light all around him (Ezek. 1:1–25). In the Ezekiel scene, the creatures and throne are described in great detail, but the "human" on the throne is given only three verses because the light is too bright (Ezek. 1:26–28). Later references make it clear that the light Paul saw was Jesus himself (Acts 9:5, 27; 22:14–15; 26:16) and his heavenly glory (2 Cor. 4:6). Now as Saul looks up, Jesus is revealed as the one on the throne. What Ezekiel could not see with clarity, Saul now beholds.

Saul is welcomed into the new community symbolically by Ananias. In Acts 9:17–19, Ananias places his hands on Saul, calling him brother. The dark state of Saul after seeing Jesus should be contrasted to Saul recovering sight. Someone from the north, the south, and now a great enemy of the church have all been welcomed.

The fourth narrative of an outcast assembled concerns Cornelius. Peter has a vision where it is revealed to him that God-fearing Gentiles (even a centurion) are welcome into the community in their Gentileness. Heavenly dreams, divine initiative, and the Spirit descending drive the narrative as Peter is drawn toward a Roman centurion. While Jews had little reason to resent those from Ethiopia, they had considerable problems with Romans, especially officers.

The decisive proof for the new order comes in triple divine dealings. First, interlocking visions of Cornelius and Peter bring them together (10:1–16). Second, Peter goes to Cornelius through the Spirit's leading (10:19–20; 11:12). Third, the Spirit is poured out on Cornelius and his household, confirming that Gentiles are brought under the lordship of Christ without having to follow Jewish rituals (10:17–48).

The final narrative concerning outcasts occurs in Antioch (11:19–30). Antioch was the third-largest city in the Roman Empire, a cosmopolitan city full of gods, and became a key mission base for Gentile outreach (13:1–4; 14:26–28; 15:22–23, 30–35). Though Jerusalem is not eclipsed, Antioch functions as the "mother church" for Gentiles. The narrative about Antioch shows the inclusion multiplies as a new *ecclesia* is birthed north of Jerusalem.

In Antioch, the disciples are first called Christians (11:26). Previously, they have been called saints, disciples, believers, brothers and sisters, the assembly, and the Way. Now outsiders label them, probably in derision. Followers of Jesus now literally "bear the name" of Christ (see Ex. 20:7).

The term "Christian" parallels Latin political terms and "further signals a shift of focus away from Judea to the larger Roman world."[9] In fact, "Christian" is a Greek word, of Latin form and Semitic background, thus encapsulating the cosmopolitan context of early Christianity.

A new name is coined for a new identity and mission. The origin of the most popular English term for Jesus followers was based on a multiethnic reality. The church is a third race; it does not obliterate distinctions but draws people together under the banner of Christ the Lord.

In 13:1, Luke identifies the leaders of this diverse community in Antioch: "Now there were in the church at Antioch prophets and teachers, Barnabas, Simeon who was called Niger, Lucius of Cyrene, Manaen a lifelong friend of Herod the tetrarch, and Saul." The extra descriptors are important.

Barnabas (a Hellenized Jew) and Saul (a Pharisee) bookend the list and will receive the attention moving forward. Three other individuals are named indicating the assorted nature of this assembly. Simeon, is also called "Niger," which is Latin for "black" and likely indicates a southern

---

9   Craig S. Keener, *Acts: An Exegetical Commentary*, vol. 2, *3:1–14:28* (Grand Rapids, MI: Baker Academic, 2012), 1848.

origin. Lucius is of Cyrene, which is in North Africa. Manaen is described as being reared with Herod the tetrarch.[10] This is the same Herod (Antipas) seen in Luke 3:1 and Acts 4:27 who conspired against Jesus. Manaen was therefore likely of "high-society," a childhood companion of the king.

Luke's list is therefore quite instructive. Saul is from Tarsus but trained as a Pharisee. Barnabas, a native of Cyprus, was a Jew of the diaspora with a priestly background. There are two black men from the south, and a man who had considerable social standing. The leaders in Antioch contained a pharisaical Jew, two men from Africa, a Hellenized Jew, and a privileged person. No wonder in Antioch they are first called "Christians."

Table 6.5   The Diverse Leaders in Antioch

Name	Hometown	Ethnicity	Social Status
Saul	Tarsus	Jew	Pharisee
Simeon	Niger	Gentile	Foreigner (black)
Lucius	Cyrenian	Gentile	Foreigner (black)
Manaen	Samaria?	Gentile/Idumean?	High-Brow
Barnabas	Cyprus	Jew	Hellenized Jew

Each of these narratives (Philip, Saul, Peter, Antioch) are vignettes of God welcoming outcasts and enfolding them into his people. God had promised he would gather others besides those already gathered (Isa. 56:8). Now God's plan comes to fruition, as the apostles preach Christ and those that receive their message are filled with the Spirt.

Gentiles Welcomed (13–28)

The restored people of God began in Jerusalem (1–7) and spread to Judea and Samaria (8–12). The next step is to take this message to predominantly Gentile territories, even if they still preach to Jews first (13–28).

Though I have divided these sections, there are precursors to this Gentile mission. The eunuch has been welcomed, Peter went into the

---

10 The word *syntrophos* means he was reared with Herod.

house of Cornelius, and the church in Antioch has been established. Yet a sanctioned mission to the Gentiles has not commenced. Acts 13–28 marks a shift with Paul's journeys and his trials.

Not every narrative will be covered in Paul's journeys. Rather, I will focus on key places that represent the welcoming of all peoples. The different areas Paul visits stand as symbols for the diverse community God builds. As there are different types of Jews, there are different types of Gentiles. All peoples are welcomed: island dwellers, the rustic, the intellectual, the religious, and the political.

Table 6.6   Key Places of Gentile Welcome in Acts 13–28

Cyprus	The Island Dwellers
Lystra	The Rustic
Philippi	Roman Households
Athens	The Philosophers/Intellectual Elite
Ephesus	The Magical/Idolaters
Rome	The Political Center

Paul's mission begins with him going to Cyprus (13:4–12). Two points about this narrative should be highlighted. First, Cyprus is an island. Like mountains, islands were viewed as irregular protrusions out of the earth and therefore stood as sites for conflict, transformation, or conversion. Fittingly, Isaiah 49:1 begins with a call from Yahweh: "Listen to me, O coastlands, / and give attention, you peoples from afar." The island dwellers are welcome.[11]

Second, at Cyprus a prominent Gentile, Sergius Paulus, comes to faith. He is an intelligent man and a governing authority, a man of high status (13:7). He is the first named Gentile convert on this mission and a prominent one who has intelligence. Therefore, on Cyprus, Luke shows the gospel message is for the high and low of society, the educated and uneducated.

---

11   Fittingly, Paul's journeys end with him on the island of Malta (Acts 28:1–10).

This point about the gospel being for all is further established by comparing and contrasting this narrative to Paul's visit to Lystra (14:8–20). Lystra is known as a backwater, rustic, and countryside town. Its people were known as mountain-dwellers.[12] This geographical and cultural reality becomes a key part of the narrative.

Paul heals a lame man like Peter did in Jerusalem (14:8–10). The crowd's response to the healing is quite different from what Peter experienced in Jerusalem, and the geographical location largely explains this divergence. In Acts 3:10, the crowd is filled with awe and astonishment, but here the crowds shout in their own language, "The gods have come down to us in the likeness of men" (14:11). This is the only time Luke refers to a local dialect outside of the Pentecost scene.

Those in Lystra think Paul and Barnabas are gods, specifically Zeus and Hermes. Instead of accepting the bulls and wreaths, the apostles tear their clothes and rush into the crowd, explaining to the people they too are creatures and not gods. They came not to introduce idolatry but destroy it.

This is an important point because many critics of Christianity accused the movement of being populated by the uneducated, whom the early missionaries had duped. However, Luke shows Paul and Barnabas don't manipulate people. They disclose their true identity and the identity of the one they worship. In Cyprus, a prominent Gentile has been welcomed; in Lystra, Paul and Barnabas have not hoodwinked those off the beaten path.

Philippi is also a significant place Paul visits because he establishes new messianic households under the thumb of Rome (16:6–40). Philippi was a Roman colony with many retired Roman soldiers. Although Paul has visited other Roman colonies, this city is highlighted for its close connection to Rome.

The emphasis on the Roman nature of this episode is evident by Luke's word choices. "Colony" is used only here and is itself a Latin loanword (16:12). The chief officials are called "magistrates" (16:20), which is a Greek term for Roman praetors. The police are called

---

12 Strabo says they lived in remote "mountain caves" and ate food "unmixed with salt" and were ignorant of the sea (Strabo *Geogr.* 12.6.5; 14.5.24, cited in Parsons, *Acts*, 200.).

rhabdouchos, which are Roman lictors (16:35), and finally Paul and Silas speak of themselves as Roman citizens (16:37–38).

These details are not merely to add local color; the narrative is concerned with the mission's penetration into the Roman world. Philippi is Rome in microcosm. And in Philippi, two household baptisms are mentioned: Lydia and the jailer. This is the first time, since Cornelius, that Luke mentions the baptism of households, which shows the success of the mission in Philippi.

Lydia becomes a central figure who hosts Paul and his companions. The jailer and his household are also converted. A rich woman and a worker of the state are welcomed. Rome valued the order of households as a microcosm of their state. Luke shows new messianic households are sprouting in the midst of a Roman colony.

If in Philippi Paul confronted Roman customs and in Lystra he challenged rustic pagan practices, then in Athens he clashes with the intellectual elite (17:16–34). Luke presents Paul as a philosopher grounded in the logic of the Hebrew Scriptures as he announces a more universal message to this sophisticated crowd.

Though many *universalize* the Athens speech, making it the training ground for every type of apologetics situation to a non-Christian crowd, the scene in Athens presses into the particular.[13] The philosophic crowd is integral to the narrative.

Even though Athens was not at its prime, it was still the center of Greek philosophy because of its association with Socrates, Plato, and Aristotle. Luke makes sure readers don't miss this point with his mention of the agora, Epicurean and Stoic philosophers, pagan shrines, and the Areopagus.

Paul addresses Athens at their basic assumptions and deploys philosophical language to stake out common ground. Though Paul is labeled an amateur philosopher (17:18), he makes Yahweh known to them through Jesus Christ. Rather than explicitly employing the Old Testament Scriptures to prove Jesus is the Messiah, as he has done at other

---

13   Eric. D. Barreto, Jacob D. Myers, and Thelathia Young, *In Tongues of Mortals and Angels: A Deconstructive Theology of God-Talk in Acts and Corinthians* (New York: Lexington Books/Fortress Academic, 2019), 45–60.

locales, Paul speaks to them in the philosophic language of the day. He quotes their own poets and alludes to their traditions. However, he does so in order to transform their worldview. The speech is essentially a call to repentance, not a search-and-find game for commonalities.

Paul narrates the incongruity between Jesus's message and Gentile religion while at the same time arguing the Christian movement contains the best features of Greek philosophy. It is the superior philosophy.

Ultimately the dividing point is Jesus's resurrection. When the Athenians hear Paul speak about the resurrection of the dead, they cut him off and mock him (17:31–32). Even though Paul's message pulled on certain commonalities, it also fundamentally challenged their social imaginary.

Many bypass this point: a church is birthed in Athens (17:32–34). Some Athenians reject Paul's message; others are interested in hearing more. A group joins Paul. Two are named: Dionysius the Areopagite and a woman named Damaris. Contrary to what some argue, Athens is not a failure. Dionysius's reception shows some from Mars Hill accepted Paul's teaching, and Damaris's close association with him may indicate Damaris is also a distinguished Areopagite.[14]

While many groups showed prejudice against women scholars in this time, some communities were more open to female members, and Epicureans and Stoics were some of these latter groups.[15] This indicates Luke paints Christianity in the same way: women scholars are welcome.

The next narrative displaying the diversity of Gentiles welcomed is Paul's work in Ephesus (18:24–19:41). Ephesus was known for its magical practices and the Artemis cult. If in Athens Paul takes on the *intellectual elite* and in Rome he goes to the *political head*, in Ephesus

---

14 Keener doubts Damaris is an Areopagite since he thinks Luke would have repeated the title. But the opposite may be the case; he did not need to repeat the title since they are associated together. Craig S. Keener, *Acts: An Exegetical Commentary*, vol. 3, *15:1–23:35* (Grand Rapids, MI: Baker Academic, 2012), 2678–80. Bede says this Dionysius was afterward ordained bishop and governed the church in Corinth and wrote many volumes. Venerable Bede, *The Venerable Bede Commentary on the Acts of the Apostles*, trans. Lawrence T. Martin (Kalamazoo, MI: Cistercian Publications, 1989), 17.34 (145).

15 F. Scott Spencer, *Journeying through Acts: A Literary-Cultural Reading* (Sheffield: Sheffield Academic Press, 1997), 183–84.

he engages in the *center of idolatry*, where he proves the forces of darkness and magic cannot overpower the name of Jesus.

Luke puts more emphasis on Paul's extraordinary miracles in this narrative than any other. He even states the handkerchiefs or aprons that touched Paul's skin were carried away and used as healing conduits (19:11–12).

Then some Jewish exorcists (sons of Sceva) try to employ Paul's power, but the evil spirits leap upon them and master them (19:13–20). Rather than displaying their power over the spirit or having the Spirit jump on them, they are overpowered, and leave defeated and shamed.

The result of this humorous incident is positive for the residents of Ephesus. Many believers confess their practices and burn their books in front of everyone (the equivalent of 50,000 days' wages). The action signals the defeat of magic by the name of Jesus: "magic has become obsolete . . . the books are emblems of a defeated regime."[16]

The effect is the word of the Lord flourished and prevailed. Here Luke reports the "growth, strength, and power" of the word (19:20, my translation) rather than multiplication, as he did in 6:7 and 9:31. This unique word choice confirms the supernatural theme in the Ephesus narrative. It signals victory for the gospel of Jesus and his community. The devil's terrain shrinks as the Lord's increases.

The final location Paul goes to is Rome: the heart of the empire. Paul has sparred with the intellectual elite, the city of magic, and the rural towns, and now he comes to the seat of power. While on trial, he testifies to kings and governors. Acts 13–28 shows the message of Jesus is available to all.

This is further supported because Rome was not the ends of the earth. Rather, it is the center of the earth (from a Roman perspective) "with a central milepost from which all the roads of the empire radiated out."[17] Though the forces of nature and the schemes of man try to stop Paul, neither can hinder God's will to welcome Gentiles.

---

16 Susan Garrett, *The Demise of the Devil: Magic and the Demonic in Luke's Writings* (Minneapolis, MN: Fortress Press, 1989), 95.

17 Loveday Alexander, *Acts in Its Ancient Literary Context: A Classicist Looks at the Acts of the Apostles*, LNTS 298 (New York: Bloomsbury T&T Clark, 2005), 214.

Excursus: The Law in Acts

As this chapter has indicated, there is a clear movement not just from Jerusalem but also seemingly away from it. This might lead some to assume that "Christianity" moves away from "Judaism" as Gentiles are brought in. However, the situation is more complex than this. In this section, we will examine Luke's view of the Jewish law in Acts.

In one sense, Acts has a congenial view of the Jewish law. Though one might be tempted to focus on the fact that the Jerusalem council does not require circumcision, interpreters are hard-pressed to bypass that everything in Acts starts in, stems from, and even returns to Jerusalem.

The first seven chapters are focused on the temple. Peter and John go to the temple at the hour of prayer, presumably to pray and speak of Jesus's resurrection (Acts 3:1). While there is critique of the Jewish leadership and the temple system, these appraisals are in hope of reform, not repudiation. It is those most zealous for the traditions who will try to reform them if they have gone awry.

As already argued, Luke portrays the apostles as the new temple people. He doesn't abandon Hebrew Bible imagery but brings it to a climax. He also paints them as those who fulfill the Torah as they share their goods (2:42–47; 4:32–37; 6:1–7). They are the ones truly adherent to the Torah as they spread life while the leaders spread death.

Stephen is accused of disrespecting the temple and the law (6:13–14), but he defends himself by giving a masterful exegesis of the Scriptures, turning the tables on his accusers, saying they are the ones who are anti-Torah. He is aligned with the maligned prophets, while they are associated with the rebellious generation.

As the book continues, the witnesses fan out past Jerusalem but continually return to Jerusalem to show that Jerusalem is still involved in the events. Paul himself gives no explicit indication that his team abandons the Torah. Luke never portrays him as an apostate Jew.

Though Paul is accused of abandoning the law (21:21, 27–28), Luke presents this accusation as clearly false. Luke has reported how Paul had Timothy circumcised (16:3), takes a Nazarite vow (18:18), observes the Feast of Unleavened Bread (20:16), and desires to observe the Festival of Weeks (20:16).

In the trials themselves, Luke portrays Paul as covenantally faithful while his opponents are faithless. Paul speaks in Hebrew (22:2), proclaims, "I am a Jew" who was educated under Gamaliel and who has been zealous for Jewish customs (22:3). Paul is a Pharisee, trained in the tradition, who honors the law and believes in the promise and hope of the nation (21:20–26; 22:1–3; 23:1, 5; 26:4–5).

To Felix, Paul says, "I worship the God of our fathers, believing everything laid down by the Law and written in the Prophets" (24:14). To Festus, he claims, "Neither against the law of the Jews, nor against the temple, nor against Caesar have I committed any offense" (25:8). To Agrippa, he states, "To this day I have had the help that comes from God, and so I stand here testifying both to small and great, saying nothing but what the prophets and Moses said would come to pass" (26:22).

His opponents bear false witness, try to murder him, take rash oaths, and form evil alliances. The unbelieving Jews are portrayed as violent, while Paul seeks reconciliation and preaches life. Paul's mission fulfills Israel's vocation to be a light to the Gentiles, but the Jews will not accept this inclusion.

Thus, Luke has a positive view of the law. This could be because he is deeply concerned with the unity and fellowship of believers, or maybe the implications of the new covenant took time to develop. Maybe readers are making more of these texts than Luke would like and some of them are more about accommodation than affirmation.

However, even if some of these are at play, it is hard to avoid Luke's friendliness to the law. Yet this must be balanced by two points. First, for Luke, the arrival of the Messiah necessitates a shift in the role of the law. In Luke's narrative, a clear transition comes in Stephen's sermon. Stephen's opponents accuse him of speaking against this holy place and Moses (6:13).

When Stephen responds, he walks through Israel's history yet also argues a new era has come. Stephen refutes the notion that the physical temple is necessary for God's presence, though it functioned as a blessing in its time. God is not and cannot be localized. Thus, the era of the physical temple is over.

The reality of the new era comes to a head when Stephen sees Jesus in the heavenly temple (7:55–56). Jesus has fulfilled the role of the temple, and now his people are mobile temples. As Greg Beale says, "to believe that Israel's temple or one rebuilt by human hands would last forever is a false view because it mistakes the symbolic temple (Heb. 9:8–10) for the real one (Heb. 9:11)."[a] Decentralizing the temple and the land provides the theological and narratival groundwork for the mission to the ends of the earth.

Thus, though the law and temple are viewed positively, they are also subsumed under the banner of Jesus. For the apostles, everything, including the law, is redrawn around Jesus Christ. As Jipp explains,

> Paul is indeed faithful to Judaism—to the people, to the Torah, and to the temple—but only in a way that is subordinate to this ultimate allegiance, namely, the resurrected

Jewish Messiah around whom Paul has oriented his entire life. Stated another way, Paul's ultimate allegiance to the resurrected Messiah results in a radical reconfiguration of the meaning of his Jewish heritage and sacred Scriptures.[b]

In this sense, the apostles do not go out proclaiming the law per se but Jesus and the law as leading to Jesus. *Luke's fundamental interest in the law is its prophetic nature.* Luke makes the most of the law when he shows it points to Jesus. The law for Luke is prophecy. It predicts the sufferings and rising of Christ. Jesus's arrival thus reconfigures the role of the law in the new era, so much so that Paul's and Peter's messages are viewed as a threat to the Jewish way of life.

Both Paul and Peter argue the meaning and significance of Israel's Scriptures and traditions come to fulfillment in Jesus the Messiah. They trace Israel's history in their speeches in such a way that defines their history as anticipating a Messiah (Acts 2, 13). When Paul is on trial, though he argues passionately that he is a Torah-observant Jew, his central claims concern the Messiah's resurrection.

Paul reinterprets his whole tradition based on the light revealed to him along the Damascus road. He thus reconfigures everything, even the Jewish law, around the Messiah. Contemporary Jews thought the Christian claim was dangerous, so they did everything they could to stamp it out because it seemed that new figures were against the law and against the people (21:21).

So does the law still hold any authority over Jews according to Luke? It does, but it is a mediated authority. Every command must run through the sieve of Jesus and ask first how the law relates to him. The law points to him and comes to fulfillment in him. While some say the apostles now replace the law as authoritative figures, it is also true that they source their authority in the Scriptures as it finds completion in Jesus.

Second, Luke's congenial view of the law must be paired with the arrival of the Spirit, who cleanses Gentiles in their *Gentileness* without them following the Torah. Gentiles don't need to follow the law. Neither *must* Jewish believers have the Mosaic law govern their behavior (though many still do follow the law).

God reveals to Peter that Gentiles are clean, signifying ritual concepts and food laws are no longer required as a separating barrier (10:1–11:18). Peter and the rest of the Jews can now have table fellowship with Gentiles. Whether that means they stopped eating kosher themselves is debated, but the vision does declare the food clean (10:13–15, 28).

At the same time, Cornelius is portrayed as a pious proselyte (10:2). Yet the amazement and resistance still reside. Despite Cornelius's piety, he remains a Gentile and therefore Peter must have three commands to convince him that he can have table fellowship with Gentiles (10:45; 11:3).

Acts 15 also gives evidence that the law is no longer a boundary for Gentiles. Gentiles are welcome into God's people without following the Torah. The debate is not about *whether* Gentiles should be accepted into Christian fellowship, but *how*.

The specific issue in the council is whether Gentiles should be required to submit to Jewish proselyte requirements (especially circumcision). Or are they free to enter the fellowship without adhering to Jewish identity markers? The answer comes in conjunction with the church's deliberation, but ultimately this has been decided by God.

Peter, Paul, and Barnabas recount what God had done through them, and James tells of what the Scriptures say. God has acted in the world. The apostles testify to the primacy and priority of God's work, not their revolution of heart. God has cleansed Gentiles. He has made the call already. They simply need to follow and believe.

However, they do ask Gentiles to follow three restrictions (15:19–20). The council writes to them, telling them to "abstain" from three things: (1) that which is polluted by idols;[c] (2) sexual immorality;[d] and (3) anything strangled and which therefore still has blood in it (cf. 15:29; 21:25).

The conglomeration of requirements has troubled interpreters because it seems to impose a collection of moral and ceremonial laws that do not naturally fit together. Four basic views are taken on the relationship between these requirements.

First, some argue these restrictions are ad hoc *moral* requirements. They are specific only to this context and reflect the things most offensive to Jewish sensibilities.

Second, others argue for a *resident aliens* perspective in reference to Leviticus 17:8–18:18, where all of these restrictions occur. Gentiles should live as if they are resident aliens among Jews and respect Jewish food laws when fellowshipping with Jews.

Third, some assert these echo traditions that became the *Noahide laws*. Latter rabbis held Gentiles responsible for keeping the requirements given to all humanity in the time of Noah. God gave six commandments to Adam, adding the prohibition of meat with blood during Noah's time (Gen. 9:4–6).

Finally, the view with the least amount of problems is that all these are associated with *pagan temple practices* and therefore idolatry. The first mention of requirements begins with the word *alisgēma* ("pollution," 15:20), which is usually associated with ritual defilement (Mal. 1:7, 12; Dan. 1:8). Table fellowship and idolatry were two sides of the same coin. Food and idolatry are linked in 1 Corinthians 10, and sexual activity was regularly found in association with meat offerings.

Table 6.7   Four Views on the Apostolic Decree in Acts 15

Moral View	Things most offensive to Jewish sensibilities in the moral sphere
Resident Alien View	Prohibitions for strangers in the land (Lev. 17–18)
Noahide Law View	The "creational" commands given to Adam and Noah
Pagan Temple View	The practices were associated with idolatry and pagan temples

Acts 15:21 supplements view four by showing these requirements should be shunned because of both personal corruption and giving offense to Jewish brothers. Therefore, the requirements regulate fellowship between the two groups *and* prevent idolatry. James says Gentiles don't need to be circumcised, but they should avoid idolatry and be sympathetic to Jews.

Gentiles don't need to start acting like Jews, and Jews don't need to start acting like Gentiles, but they should be compassionate and understanding to both perspectives and watch out for idolatry. Jews can practice the faith in their way, and Gentiles can as well—but all need to be washed in love. Distinguishing what is necessary and what is periphery is paramount for Christian fellowship.

Therefore, while Luke has a positive portrayal of the law, he also acknowledges that Gentiles are clean and welcome without adhering to the Torah. God has made them clean. The Scriptures have testified to the growth of David's family. And the Spirit has fallen on them before they were circumcised.

Luke thus seems to affirm three things at once about the law. First, Paul and the other Jewish apostles are faithful Jews, Torah-observant. Second, and most importantly, the Jewish law is reconfigured around the Messiah. He takes priority and everything must be interpreted through him. The law is primarily prophetic in Acts. Third, because Jesus has arrived and the Spirit has been poured out, Gentiles are welcome in their *Gentileness*. God has made them clean. As Craig Blomberg concludes, "the Law was not abolished but it was no longer directly relevant for the church *apart from* its fulfillment in and interpretation by the Lord Jesus."[e]

a   G. K. Beale, *The Temple and the Church's Mission: A Biblical Theology of the Dwelling Place of God*, NSBT (Downers Grove, IL: IVP Academic, 2004, 297.

b   Joshua Jipp, *Reading Acts*, Cascade Companions (Eugene, OR: Cascade Books, 2018), 116.

c   Things polluted by idols could refer to a range of things, but it is especially employed in reference to food and drink dedicated to other gods (Dan. 1:8; Mal. 1:7, 12; 1 Cor. 8–10).

d   In Jewish tradition, sexual immorality and idolatry were closely associated (Hos. 5:3–4; Ezek. 16:15–46; Jer. 3:1–10; Wis. 14:12, 24; *Jub.* 22:16–23; 1 Cor. 10:7–8; Rev. 2:14, 20).

e   Craig L. Blomberg, "The Law in Luke-Acts," *JSNT*, 7 no. 22 (1984): 72.

Conclusion

The church, the new people of God, is a major theme in Acts. God's plan all along was to form a community that bore his name and image. Members of this community are sometimes called holy, emphasizing their identity and character; sometimes disciples, indicating their connection to Jesus; sometimes brothers and sisters, demonstrating the breakdown of normal social barriers; sometimes the Way, indicating their new rule of life; and sometimes Christians, emphasizing their multiethnic identity.[18]

The church is not a side story to God's work in the world. It does not sit on the bench as the clock ticks on. Rather, the church is central to God's plan. If people want to be caught up in what God is doing

18   Seccombe, "The New People of God."

in the world, then the stage upon which this play is unfolding is the church. The church is the hotspot where God works, where his glory is displayed. God came to rescue a people and teach them how to walk in his ways.

In the above chapter, I have traced the narrative expansion of the people of God. It all began in Jerusalem as Israel was renewed. God's people were established at Pentecost and by the power of the Spirit continue to grow (Acts 1–7). Stephen's climactic speech provided the theological and narratival impetus for God's people to scatter to the outcasts (Acts 8–12). Then, the church grew through welcoming outcasts and Gentiles in various cities that represented diverse beliefs, lifestyles, philosophies, and loyalties (Acts 13–28).

However, a reader would be mistaken to think this expansion was at the impetus of God's people. God's people are continually catching up to the Spirit's work. He pushes them along. The triune God spurs on growth. He turns their blood into greater life. He changes their enthnocentrism to inclusion. He reveals visions to them. He pushes them farther than they would ever go on their own. This is God's work, his economy, his plan.

Jesus is no longer on the earth, but his Spirit fills his followers, and a new body is formed. Acts recounts not only the church's establishment but also its witness. It is to this theme we turn more fully in the next chapter.

Witness to the Ends of the Earth

*"You will be my witnesses in Jerusalem and in all
Judea and Samaria, and to the end of the earth."*

ACTS 1:8

Ring of Fire

Johnny Cash, the famous American singer-songwriter, popularized
the song "Ring of Fire." The lyrics sound ominous and painful, as
he speaks about plunging into a "burning ring of fire." However,
the song is about Cash's love for June Carter. Cash says his love for
Carter is like a burning thing, and he is bound by wild desire. "It
burns, burns, burns."

Acts is like Cash's burning ring of fire. The Spirit descends as fire,
compelling people to witness and tell of the life-giving presence of God.
The Spirit's power envelops the apostles, and the flames go higher and
higher. The ring of fire expands.

Based on the centrality of Acts 1:8, many thematic studies and
sermon series on Acts view "witnessing" as the central theme. A
quick Google search displays sermon subtitles such as "To the Ends
of the Earth" or "Empowered for Jesus's Mission" or "You Will Be
My Witnesses."

Most agree the key verse for understanding the narrative of Acts is 1:8, where the apostles are called to be witnesses.[1] This verse details the main commission and outline for the book. The apostles are the master storytellers who witness to the reality of divine presence upon the earth. Yet the foundation for this mission is sometimes assumed.

The theme of "witnessing to the ends of earth" does not occur unless God the Father had planned it long ago, Christ the Son is exalted, the Spirit is poured out, and the church is established. To put this another way, mission cannot occur unless God compels and gathers his people. Global witness, a major theme of Acts, is built on the footing of other realities.

Having said all that, it is still true that Acts has a relentless focus on witnessing.[2] No other book narrates the spread of the gospel like Acts. No other book describes the church's early activities like Acts. No other book (besides the Johannine literature) uses the term or concept "witness" as much as Acts.

The exalted Jesus sovereignly directs the church's witness through the Spirit's empowering so that his servants can spread the word of salvation to the nations. The Father and Son work from heaven, but their troops are on the ground. These witnesses will progress through pain, persecution, and preaching.

Table 7.1   Witness in Acts

What?	They witness to the life-giving presence of God in Jesus Christ.
Who?	The twelve apostles witness as representatives of God's people.
To Whom and How?	They witness to the ends of the earth by suffering like the servant.

1   I use the title *witness* here, rather than *mission*, because in Acts witness refers to the activity of humans, while mission primarily refers to the work of God. Bolt made me aware of this distinction. Peter G. Bolt, "Mission and Witness," in *Witness to the Gospel: The Theology of Acts*, ed. I. Howard Marshall and David Peterson (Grand Rapids, MI: Eerdmans, 1998), 191.

2   Rowe rightly challenges the idea that there was never any kind of mission in Judaism prior to Christianity, but it is correct to affirm there never was a Jewish mission of the kind we see in Acts prior to Christianity. C. Kavin Rowe, *World Upside Down: Reading Acts in the Graeco-Roman Age* (Oxford: Oxford University Press, 2010), 119.

I will cover three questions in this section: What does it mean to witness? Who were the witnesses? To whom and how were they to witness?

What?

What does it mean to be a witness? In a legal sense, to witness means to tell of facts. Someone "witnesses" to a crime or "witnesses" in court. In the religious sense, people still use the term "witness" for evangelism.

In Acts, the meaning of witness hails from Isaiah and Exodus. In Exodus, *martys* (witness) is the word of choice for the ark of the "testimony" (Ex. 25:22) and the tent of "meeting" (Ex. 29:4). The Ten Commandments are called the two tablets of witness written by the finger of God (Ex. 31:18; 32:15). Noticeably, there is a distinct focus on God's covenant, presence, and word.

God "witnesses" to his own presence in the tabernacle and over the ark in the Ten Commandments. His presence is found where his word is found. He has given his presence to his people in the covenant document. The presence of God is life-giving to those who walk according to his covenant.

God's life-giving presence was never meant to be hoarded by Israel but to spread to the world. But Israel could never fulfill this reality. Rather than providing clarity, they continually distorted their understanding of God with their sin.

The prophet Isaiah picks up these themes and expands upon them. Luke is clearly indebted to Isaiah and his understanding of what it means to be a witness. This can be seen in the clustering of texts from Isaiah alluded to in Acts 1:8 (see table 7.2).

Isaiah contrasts Israel with the nations. The nations worship gods that are deaf and blind. They serve that which is not alive, but Yahweh is the "I am who I am" (Ex. 3:14)—the ever living one and the Creator of all things.

God calls the nations to witness to him in a cosmic trial, but they cannot, so he calls Israel as his witness since they have been chosen to testify to his life-giving presence (Isa. 43:8–10; 44:8–12). The servant (Isa. 43:10; 49:6), Israel, and the Davidic King (Isa. 55:4) are the true witnesses.

Table 7.2   Witness in Isaiah

Isaiah 43:10: "*You are my witnesses,*" declares the LORD, "and my servant whom I have chosen, that you may know and believe me and understand that I am he. Before me no god was formed, nor shall there be any after me."

Isaiah 43:12: "I declared and saved and proclaimed, when there was no strange god among you; *and you are my witnesses,*" declares the LORD, "and I am God."

Isaiah 44:8: "Fear not, nor be afraid; have I not told you from of old and declared it? *And you are my witnesses!* Is there a God besides me? There is no Rock; I know not any."

Isaiah 49:6: "It is too light a thing that you should be my servant to raise up the tribes of Jacob and to bring back the preserved of Israel; I will make you as a light for the nations, that my salvation may reach *to the end of the earth.*"

Therefore, in both Exodus and Isaiah, God calls his people to witness to his life-giving presence. They are to tell all people that there is no God like Yahweh (Isa. 43:10). They are to say that their God is from of old (Isa. 44:8).

Acts picks up on these themes, as God calls Israel to witness God's abundant life. Many of these testimonies are given in an *actual courtroom* (echoing Isaiah). In Acts, the difference from the Old Testament is the specificity of the witness. No longer do the people testify only to Yahweh, but to Yahweh revealed in Jesus Christ. The apostles witness to the resurrection life of Jesus brought to earth by the power of the Spirit.

The focus on the "Jesus event" is what readers find in the apostles' witness speeches, but a special emphasis lies on the resurrection. When the apostles are selecting another apostle, they say "one of these men must become with us a witness to his resurrection" (Acts 1:22).

When Peter preaches his Pentecost sermon, he affirms they are witnesses to the raising up of Jesus (2:32). While the Jerusalem leaders killed the Author of life, it was God who raised him from the dead, and they are witnesses to this (3:15; 4:33; 5:32). Peter testifies to Cornelius of Jesus's death and resurrection (10:39–41).

Paul, likewise, in his first sermon proclaims that after a long period of preparation (13:16–25), the word of salvation has come to the world in the person of Jesus Christ. Jesus will never see decay (13:35), for he has been exalted above all. Paul testifies to Athens of Jesus's resurrection (17:18), and in his trials he continually returns to Jesus's new life (23:6; 24:15, 21; 28:20).

The apostles are thus "Jesus's authorized delegates, witnesses to the reality of his resurrection and expounders of its significance."[3] In Acts, to witness means *to see and tell of the life-giving presence of God found in Jesus Christ through the Spirit.*

Who?

The term "witness" (*martys*) is largely reserved for the twelve apostles in Luke's writings (Luke 24:48; Acts 1:8; 1:22; 2:32; 3:15; 5:32; 10:39, 41), but these men stand as representatives for the people of God.[4] They are the new Israel and the servants Isaiah spoke of in his writings (Isa. 43:10; 49:6).

The apostles play a relatively minor role in Luke, compared to Matthew and Mark, most likely anticipating their major role in Acts. As Luke's two-part narrative unfolds, the apostles become the bridge between the ministry of Jesus in his Gospel and the witness of the church in Acts. They can witness because they have seen the risen Jesus, both physically and spiritually. Christ has opened their eyes to the realities foretold in the Scriptures: the Messiah will suffer, rise, and be enthroned, and repentance and forgiveness of sins will be proclaimed to all nations. "You are witnesses of these things" (Luke 24:44–49). Therefore, the apostles witness to the fulfillment of the covenant in the life, crucifixion, and exaltation of Christ because they were witnesses to the Jesus event (Luke 24:48; Acts 1:8).

The emphasis on the number of the apostles is important because the twelve symbolize God's people who witness to the nations. Though

---

3 Andrew C. Clark, "The Role of the Apostles," in Howard and Peterson, *Witness to the Gospel*, 178.

4 Stephen is also labeled a witness (Acts 22:20).

Acts focuses more on the witness of the apostles than of the church more broadly, the apostles stand as representative ideal characters whom the church emulates. Stephen, a Hellenized Jew, is also a witness, and Paul becomes a witness who goes to the ends of the earth. Interestingly, both Stephen and Paul also see the risen Jesus (Acts 7:56; 9:5–6).

Two main "witnesses" receive the bulk of attention in Acts: Peter and Paul. Peter is the first key witness, and Luke's pen follows him for around half of the narrative. However, Peter also seems to stand as representative of the collective apostolic group (2:14, 37, 42; 3:4, 12; 4:7, 13, 19; 5:2–3, 29; 6:2; 8:14–20).[5] Continually, a companion or the apostles join Peter, and a new witness steps onto the scene in the second half: Paul. Paul is an authorized witness to all men (13:31; 22:14–15; 26:16), but he too is accompanied by companions. He is not inferior to the apostles; indeed, Luke does call him an apostle along with Barnabas (14:4, 14).

However, Luke seems most often to shy away from using capital "A" apostle, as it were, in reference to Paul, reserving it for the twelve. Paul's distinction is based on his time and function rather than rank.[6] This is evident in the abundant parallels between Peter's ministry in the first half of the book and Paul's in the second.

Luke summarizes their miraculous deeds in similar ways (2:43; 5:12; 14:3; 15:12). Both heal the lame (3:1–10; 14:8–10), bring the dead back to life (9:36–43; 20:9–12), experience miracles of liberation (12:3–17; 16:25–34), fall into trances (10:10; 22:17), and are involved in incidents with supernatural punishments (5:1–11; 13:8–

---

5   Hans F. Bayer, "The Preaching of Peter in Acts," in *Witness to the Gospel*, 261.

6   Talbert notes, "In the period AD 80–100, there remains the same distinction between apostles of Christ and apostles of the churches. Luke-Acts speaks about apostles of Christ in Luke 6:13; Acts 1:2, 26; 2:37, 42, 43; 4:33, 35; 5:2; 5:18; 6:6; 8:18; 15:2, 22, 23; 16:4 (cf. 13:31). Acts 14:4, 14 (cf. 13:1–3) refer to apostles of a church, Antioch of Syria. In this dominant schema of Luke-Acts, the Twelve are viewed as apostles of Christ; Paul and Barnabas are viewed as apostles of the church in Antioch of Syria." But Talbert also notes Paul is seen as an apostle of Christ. Charles H. Talbert, *Reading Acts: A Literary and Theological Commentary* (Macon, GA: Smyth & Helwys, 2013), 16–17.

12). One poignant similarity is that both have inaugural speeches quoting Psalm 16:10 (Acts 2:13–26; 13:16–41). Peter and Paul thus stand as representative witnesses for the church as a whole. The numerous parallels between Peter and Paul legitimize Paul's mission to the world.[7]

Table 7.3 Parallels between Peter and Paul

Peter	Paul
Sermon (2:22–39)	Sermon (13:26–41)
Healing a paralytic (3:1–10)	Healing a paralytic (14:8–11)
Filled with the Spirit for ministry (4:8)	Filled with the Spirit for ministry (13:9)
Indirect healings (5:15)	Indirect healings (19:12)
Defended by a Pharisee in the Sanhedrin (5:34–39)	Defended by Pharisees in the Sanhedrin (23:9)
Appoints leaders through laying on hands (6:1–6)	Appoints leaders through laying on hands (19:6)
People receive the Spirit through his hands (8:17)	People receive the Spirit through his hands (19:6)
Raises the dead (9:36–41)	Raises the dead (20:9–12)
Befriends centurion (10:24–48)	Befriends centurion (27:1–44)
Defends Gentile mission in Jerusalem (11:4–17; 15:7–11)	Defends Gentile mission in Jerusalem (15:4; 21:21–26; 22:21)
Imprisoned at a Jewish festival (12:4–7)	Imprisoned at a Jewish festival (22:24; cf. 20:16)
Miraculous release from prison (5:19; 12:6–11)	Miraculous release from prison (16:25–34)

So who are the witnesses in Acts? The witnesses are the twelve. Stephen and Paul are included, but all of them stand as representative figures. The twelve stand for Israel, Stephen as the Hellenized witness, and Paul as the missionary to Gentiles. They have seen the risen Lord Jesus and they spread the life of Jesus to all people.

7 This chart is largely taken from Craig S. Keener, *Acts: An Exegetical Commentary*, vol. 1, *Introduction and 1:1–2:47* (Grand Rapids, MI: Baker Academic, 2012), 562.

Where and How?

To witness means to see and tell of the life-giving presence of Jesus. The twelve apostles and Paul are designated primarily for this task, but they are representative figures for those who have experienced Jesus. Now the question becomes, *Where* are they to witness and *how* will they go about this task?

Although it can be tempting to simply say "to the ends of the earth" as noted in the previous chapter, the apostles have an Israel-first mission. Acts 1:8 details this progression. They are to witness in Jerusalem first, then in Judea and Samaria, and then to the ends of the earth. The Gentile mission develops only after Israel has heard.

Table 7.4   The Scope of the Apostles' Witness

Jerusalem >>>>>> Judea and Samaria >>>>>> the ends of the earth

A closer look at this progression might provide more confusion than clarity, as Judea is the larger region in which Jerusalem is found, and Acts 8–12 doesn't merely recount mission in Judea and Samaria: Antioch, Syria, Damascus, and Jerusalem are also included in 8–12. What, then, does Luke mean by this progression?

The answer can be found in that "Judea" stands for the land of Israel, more holistically including what was then Roman Syria.[8] Luke can use Judea in both a more proper way (the southern district of Palestine distinct from Galilee; 9:31) and a more general way (encompassing all Palestine; 10:37).

The gospel goes from the more narrow Jerusalem to the wider area called Judea and Samaria. Judea and Samaria is a merism covering that entire region. The two regions are linked grammatically and include the adjectival modifier "all."

The last phrase "the end of the earth" is also debated. Does it refer to Rome or something else? Early literature refers to Rome as the ends of the

---

8   Martin Hengel, "Ἰουδαία in the Geographical List of Acts 2:9–11 and Syria as 'Greater Judea,'" *BBR* 10, no. 2 (2000): 161–80.

earth, but the ancients knew of lands beyond Rome. For ancient people, these limits lay at the Atlantic, by the Germans, Scythians, Indians, and Ethiopians. Deuteronomy 28:49 refers to Babylon as the end of the earth, and an early geographer/historian refers to Spain as the ends of the earth.

The shape of Luke's narrative in Acts indicates that readers should see Rome as representative of the whole world. The mission is not over when it reaches Rome, but Rome provides a base for the gospel going to the ends of the earth. As noted earlier, this order (Jerusalem, Judea and Samaria, and to the ends of the earth) is not only geographical but also theopolitical (Jesus the King—Caesar).[9]

Acts not only alludes to the Old Testament but also challenges the power of the Roman Empire. Rome made her empire safe and navigable for the celebration and spread of her *paideia*. Luke's implication is that God will create another empire parallel to Roman rule.[10]

However, to claim that this new empire is political might confuse readers. The witnesses come not with swords, bows, and shields but as *suffering servants*. They witness not only in word but also in deed. They embody a cross-shaped way of being in the world, conforming to their message. "Acts does not construe 'witness' monothematically as the proclamation of Jesus' resurrection . . . but more comprehensively as living out the pattern of life that culminates in resurrection."[11] They not only preach Christ's death and resurrection but embody it.

As we have already seen in this chapter, Isaiah connects being a witness to being God's suffering servants in Isaiah 43:10 and 49:6:

"You *are my witnesses*," declares the LORD, "*and my servant* whom I have chosen, that you may know and believe me and understand that I am he. Before me no god was formed, nor shall there be any after me." (Isa. 43:10)

---

9   The ethnic reading is supported by both the allusions to Isaiah and the intertextual connection with Matt. 28:19, where Jesus calls his disciples to go out to all "nations."
10 Laura Salah Nasrallah, "The Acts of the Apostles, Greek Cities, and Hadrian's Panhellenion," *JBL* 127, no. 3 (2008): 533–66.
11 Rowe, *World Upside Down*, 153.

"It is too light a thing that you should be *my servant* to raise up the tribes of Jacob and to bring back the preserved of Israel; I will make you as a light for the nations, that my salvation may reach *to the end of the earth*." (Isa. 49:6)

To be a witness is to be God's servant who brings salvation to the ends of the earth. Holly Beers even argues that all of Acts portrays God's people as carrying out the mission of the suffering servant.[12] The apostles's messages, suffering, nonviolent responses, vindications, and vocabulary all mark them as the new servants. The servant themes can be seen in each of the large blocks of the Acts narrative as Luke employs various echoes to Isaiah's literature.

In Acts 1–7, the suffering servant images and terms abound. The lame man leaps (Acts 3:8; cf. Isa. 35:6), Peter identifies Jesus as "the Righteous One" (Acts 3:14; cf. Isa. 53:11), and the apostles label themselves witnesses (Acts 3:15; 4:33; cf. Isa. 43:10) and servants (Acts 4:29; cf. Isa. 49:3). David is labeled servant (Acts 4:25; cf. Isa. 37:35), as is Jesus (Acts 3:13, 26; 4:27, 30). Peter's message describes Jesus with words like "glorified" (Acts 3:13; cf. Isa. 52:13), "exalted" (Acts 5:31; cf. Isa. 52:13), and "handed over" (Acts 3:13; cf. Isa. 53:6, 12). Then the apostles suffer and are persecuted (Acts 3:18; 4:1–3; cf. Isa. 52:13–53:12), but they are innocent, supporting nonviolent responses (Acts 4:29–31, 33; 6:12–15; 7:57–60).

The servant theme continues, even in the non-apostles in Acts 8–12. The most obvious is the quotation of Isaiah 53:7–8 in 8:32–33, when the eunuch asks who Isaiah speaks of. Paul also is commissioned to suffer (Acts 9:16; cf. Isa. 52:13–53:12), and James's death in Acts 12:2 parallels that of the ultimate servant (Isa. 53:8), while Peter is handed over (Acts 12:4; cf. Isa. 53:6, 12).

Paul's ministry in Acts 13–20 is also filled with servant echoes. He takes up the servant mantle both positively (Acts 13:31; cf. Isa. 43:10;

---

12 The next three paragraphs are dependent on Holly Beers, *The Followers of Jesus as the "Servant": Luke's Model from Isaiah for the Disciples in Luke-Acts* (London: Bloomsbury T&T Clark, 2016).

Acts 13:32; cf. Isa. 61:1; Acts 15:7; cf. Isa. 41:8–9) and negatively (Acts 13:45; 14:2, 4–5, 19; 17:5–9, 13; 18:5–6, 12, 17, 19:8–9; cf. Isa 49:4; 50:6–9; 53:2–3; 66:5). The gospel goes to Jews and Gentiles (Isa. 42:6; 49:6–7; 52:15), and new exodus imagery, which is connected to the work of the servant (Acts 13:10–11; 14:8–10; 16:17; 18:15–16; 19:9, 23), is continually employed.

In Acts 21–28, Paul suffers (Acts 21:11, 31–33; 22:4; cf. Isa 53:6, 12), he is rejected by Jews (Acts 23–25), Gentiles hear and welcome him (Acts 27–28; cf. Isa. 40:5; 42:6; 49:6; 66:18–23), he is chosen and a witness (Acts 22:14–15; 23:11; 26:16, 22; cf. Isa. 42:1; 43:10), he is innocent (Acts 23:9; 23:29; 25:7, 8, 10–11, 25; 26:31–32; 28:17–18; cf. Isa 50:7–9; 53:4–6, 8–12), and the Isaianic new exodus language continues (Acts 22:4; 24:14, 22; 26:18).

In summary, to witness in Acts is to act as a suffering servant following the true suffering servant, not only in word but also in action. Christ's witnesses die but rise. They are shamed yet honored. They are castigated yet innocent. Paul and the rest of the witnesses go to trial because of the resurrection and ascension of Christ.

They not only proclaim the death of their Messiah but also are willingly delivered into death's hands. They walk into the lion's den proclaiming the lordship of Jesus, knowing that even if they are not rescued, he will raise them up on the last day.

Conclusion

Acts is unique in the Bible in that it catalogues the spread of the gospel to various regions. The twelve apostles and Paul carry this message to the surrounding regions. According to the Old Testament, to witness means to speak of God's life-giving presence in his covenantal word. This is in distinction from the gods of the nations who are deaf and dumb. In Acts, this message receives specificity as the apostles identify that Jesus Christ is the fullest revelation of this life-giving hope.

The sermons in Acts therefore trace Israel's history, centering on Jesus's movement from death to life and from suffering to exaltation.

Jesus provides life by sacrifice. Isaiah predicted this is what the servant would do. It is no surprise, therefore, that as the book of Acts unfolds, the "body of Jesus" acts like their head.

The apostles witness not only in word but also in deed. They become the new servants who spread life through the death of their own bodies. They are castigated, imprisoned, and put on trial. However, their message is always that life reverberates in Jesus's resurrection.

As will be explained in the conclusion, this mission is not complete. Witnessing and mission are tasks not complete until Jesus returns. We too are called to be God's servants, his ambassadors, his delegates, who tell everyone we meet about the hope we have found. Mission is not one of the many "programs" of God's people but the very telos of their existence.

Acts is a book about witnessing. This was God's plan. This was what Jesus sent his followers to do. This is what the Holy Spirit empowered them for. And they witness to the ends of the earth.

Conclusion

Renewal through Retrieval

God's Plan

I have argued Acts concerns the mission of the triune God. The Father's plan was to bless Israel and the nations through his Son. The Son came, died, was raised, and ascended. Then they both poured out the Spirit, thus forming a new community. Now the new community goes out and witnesses to the triune God's offer of life.

Canadian rapper Drake sings about God's plan and pairs it with "bad things" that occur.[1] In Acts, God's plan is combined with bad things happening to God's people. Persecution is a major part of Acts. Though I have not put it as a separate theme, it has been woven into each chapter. Lurking beneath the surface of each theme is a dark side.

The Father's plan is contested by Satan and the world. The Son's life is countered by death. The Spirit's work is challenged by demonic forces. The word progresses despite persecution. Salvation goes to all flesh despite ethnocentrism. The church is established despite the failures of God's people. And they witness to the ends of the earth despite the hardships they encounter. Acts encourages the people of God as they endure trials.

I began this book by stating Acts is not only a transitional book but also a programmatic one. It has something to teach every generation.

---

1 Drake, "God's Plan," *Scorpion* (Young Money, Cash Money, Republic, 2018).

We must follow its model. It is not a book locked up in the past but bursting with meaning for the present. As Erasmus says, Acts provides "the foundations of the newborn church . . . through [which] we hope that the church in ruins will be reborn."[2]

The last words of Acts indicate the narrative is incomplete:

> [Paul] lived there two whole years at his own expense, and welcomed all who came to him, proclaiming the kingdom of God and teaching about the Lord Jesus Christ with all boldness and without hindrance. (28:30–31)

Most stories enjoy tying all the loose ends together, while others leave things unfinished for readers to consider their own responsibility.[3] Luke closes his narrative with abruptness: a two-verse summary of Paul's prison ministry in Rome.

What Luke does not recount is almost as notable as what he does. He does not relate Paul's audience with Caesar, Paul's release, or the response to Paul's message. Rather, he communicates the time Paul spent in the rented house (two years), his hospitality (he welcomed all—most likely Jews and Gentiles), and the success of his message (proclaiming the kingdom of God and the Lord Jesus Christ with all boldness and without hindrance).

This shows Luke's account is not about Paul or Peter primarily, but about God's work in the world. Acts is about resurrection life, the expansion of the temple, and the advance of the word. While Paul is in prison, the testimony of Jesus and the kingdom go forth unhindered.

2　Desiderius Erasmus, *Paraphrase on Acts*, trans. Robert D. Sider, vol. 50 of *Collected Works of Erasmus* (Toronto: University of Toronto Press, 1995), 4.

3　Joshua Jipp, *Divine Visitations and Hospitality to Strangers in Luke-Acts: An Interpretation of the Malta Episode in Acts 28:1–10* (Leiden: Brill, 2013), 284–87, argues this entire last section and not just the last few verses of Acts has an open-endedness to it. This explains why Luke resorts to symbols in this last section rather than being more explicit. By excluding information (e.g., explicit preaching of the gospel, explicit Eucharist meal), Luke displaces his reader, leaves the narrative open, and calls his readers to participate in the narrative.

The last word of the book, *akōlytōs* ("unhindered"), confirms there were no restraints on Paul's preaching. Luke has already employed a form of this word (*kōlyō*) at key junctures three times in his narrative. It occurs in the story of the eunuch (8:36) and twice in the Cornelius narrative (10:47; 11:17). The gospel of the risen and ascended Lord Jesus has overcome all geographic boundaries, social differences, ethnic diversities, human prejudices, gender biases, legal obstacles, and theological barriers.[4]

This abrupt but victorious ending compels readers to ask about their own role in this narrative. Acts offers a word of encouragement. Yet, encouragement for what? The last two sentences indicate it is an encouragement to press on in the mission. The triune God is doing a work in the world that the powers of darkness marvel at, and the world will both oppose and be astonished at it. Though there will be setbacks, though all might seem dark, though it might seem as if God's people are always in the valley, a light shines through the gloom. God's purposes will not be stopped. They will not be stopped because God has pledged himself to this work. He has put his name behind it.

Acts is therefore a programmatic book because it encourages the church to press on in its own agency as it is compelled by divine agency. God is building his church. Therefore, the church must welcome all, speak of salvation in Jesus's name, and witness to the ends of the earth.

Though Luke's narrative is finished, the opportunities for his hearers are endless. The church narrative and God's mission continue. They expand toward the horizon. A retrieval of the theology of Acts provides the groundwork for the rebirth of the modern church. Since Luke wrote an ordered narrative, readers must follow this order to mine the theological rebirth that Luke offers.

Seven Themes for Renewal

We have looked at seven themes that encompass much of the theology of Acts. Each of these is a renewal stream that the modern church can

---

4   Richard Pervo, *Acts: A Commentary*, Hermeneia (Minneapolis, MN: Fortress Press, 2008), 688, notes in Greek literature and the philosophical tradition the term *akōlytōs* is related to virtue.

drink deeply from. The first three themes dealt with the triune God. The core belief Christians have confessed is our God is one God in three persons. This is the foundation of the theology of Acts; no, the foundation of all theology.

All doctrine flows *from*, *through*, and *to* this reality (Rom. 11:36). Any theology of Acts that neglects a Trinitarian reading neglects a Christian reading of Acts. Evangelicals like to speak of the gospel and missions, but less consistently defend and define Trinitarian parameters. A theology of Acts helps put the Father, Son, and Spirit front and center again and also confirms their eternal relations of origin. It is fitting that the Father plans, the Son is the begotten one, and the Spirit proceeds from the Father and Son.

First, we looked at the Father's actions in Acts. Though the Father doesn't usually receive much attention in studies on Acts, the Father is the one who orchestrates all action. The neglect of the Father's actions in Acts betrays a misguided emphasis in the church. Sometimes the church has prioritized second- or third-tier theological issues. We forget the main thing—God himself.

For most of Christian history, the doctrine of God, life with God, and thought about God were paramount and the ballast for health and renewal. More specifically, a theology of the Father has in modern times downplayed (or even denied) two key doctrines of God found in Acts: sovereignty and immutability. Without these theological cornerstones Acts doesn't make sense.

The sovereignty of God means he controls all things. All action in Acts stems from the Fathers' orchestration. He is *The Sovereign*. He directs, guides, and fulfills his promises. He has a plan, and that plan will come to pass because not a single atom falls outside of his will. He also directs every step of the church. He sovereignly propels the growth of the church. He is present in every action, every persecution, every death, every conversion.

Acts focuses on not only the sovereignty of God but also the immutability of God. Immutability means God does not change. Acts was written to encourage the church because God is the one who fulfills his promises. God does not evolve, progress, or develop. He made promises to his people about a Messiah and their future, and these will come to pass.

He fulfills his promises because he is the perfect being in whom there is no shift or variation. No matter what the church encounters, it can trust God will do what he has promised because he is not like a man that he should change his mind.

Second, we also looked at the exalted Christ who now lives and rules. Readers of Acts throughout history have focused on the Spirit, but Christ has a stubborn presence in Acts. Evangelicals in particular have tended to focus on Christ's death or his return. Acts steps in and corrects this imbalance. Luke, in his second volume, puts his eyes on the victory of Jesus: his resurrection and ascension.

The exaltation of Jesus is the culmination—even climax—of his work. Without the resurrection-ascension, the cross is a tragedy. Christianity exists, the New Testament exists, Acts exists, because Jesus is Lord. This is the apostle's message. This is our gospel.

Acts reminds us that Christ continues to work in the present. Christ is alive and working now. He acts from heaven. He directs. He guides. He compels. Yet, his victory doesn't mean all is well. The church awaits the manifestation of his reign in full. Therefore, we preach a reigning Christ, even as we continue to be a sojourning and exiled people.

Christ's exaltation helps us remember the reality of present hope and keeps our theology grounded and longing for our full inheritance. As John Calvin reminds us, the church is not promised it will "lead a joyous and peaceful life, have rich possessions, be safe from all harm. . . . No, our happiness belongs to the heavenly life!"[5] The exalted Christ causes the church to remember its hope is eternally secure, but life on earth can still be full of questions and hardships.

Third, we examined the Spirit's work in Acts. Christians have historically had a complicated relationship with the Spirit. It seems that

---

5   John Calvin, *Institutes of the Christian Religion*, ed. John T. McNeill, trans. Ford Lewis Battles (Philadelphia, PA: Westminster, 1960), 2.15.4 (498).

some traditions overspeak about the Spirit, while others are content to ignore the Spirit. Acts comes along and balances on the tightrope.

The Spirit is ever active in Acts, applying salvation, establishing the church, and empowering for mission. The Spirit is not a second blessing, but the blessing Christ secures. We live in the Spirit age. Pentecost can never be taken away. Any tradition that downplays the work of the Spirit must return to the theology of Acts.

Acts teaches us that resurrection life is here through the Spirit. Wind and fire spread across the world, spreading new creation. Pentecost is not repeatable, but it is also not retractable. The power of the Spirit is present and cannot be taken away. Any renewal movement must submit itself to the Spirit's work in its midst.

The Spirit's work is multiform in Acts, but two evidences of the Spirit's work can be highlighted here. First, the Spirit compels boldness in speaking of Jesus. The Spirit is also always pointing back to the work of Jesus. He is the "shy" third person of the Trinity whose mission is always to exalt Christ. A truly Christ-centered movement will be Spirit-filled. A Spirit-filled movement will be Christ-centered. Second, the Spirit compels the church to share her resources. The Spirit is attentive to and involved with the economic practices of the church. One clear indication of the Spirit's work in a body of believers is their generosity to the needy.

The fourth theme we traced was the progress and spread of the word in Acts. Any renewal in church history has been accompanied by a return to the covenant documents where an explanation of the gospel is found.

In Acts, the word becomes a divine character who runs out ahead of the apostles. In a real sense, the word does the work. The word grows, multiplies, and has power. Acts informs the modern-day church that a truly "word-focused" ministry will not be dead or inert, but ever active. The word compels growth. The word drives multiplication. The word is inherently powerful. A word-centered church that is not a growing church is an oxymoron. The two intertwine in Acts. Even more than that, the word compels growth.

In an age when churches seek the biggest personalities, Acts reminds us growth comes *from* and *through* the word. The apostles were amazing; their clothes healed people. But they are all dead. Only their message continues. A revival in the church will stop looking at leaders and begin looking more to the word. The power is in the message. Renewal begins with a retrieval of the centrality of the word.

Fifth, we looked at the theme of salvation to all flesh. God's mission is to rescue his people. Rome is not the main enemy. Nor are Republicans, Democrats, Liberals, Conservatives, Arabs, Muslims, or South Americans. What we all need rescue from is Satan, sin, death, and the world. All humanity has the same enemies. Renewal in the church will therefore rightly identify antagonists.

Sin and satanic forces spread division among God's people. However, Jesus has defeated sin, death, and Satan. Salvation is here. While the modern church has the tendency to view salvation in the realm of "spirituality," in Acts salvation is multidimensional.

Salvation includes body, soul, and social status. It involves incorporation into a new community: status-inversion. The lowly are raised up and promised liberation. Evangelicals have narrowed "salvation" unduly. A theology of Acts recovers a more multicolored salvation theology.

Sixth, we saw how the church was established in Acts. God gathers a people into a community. He sent Christ into the world not only to save individuals but to save *a* community of people and to save people *into* a community. The Spirit comes to a gathered group of people at Pentecost. Any renewal today will have a strong emphasis on the church. Though God certainly meets with his people at any place and time, there is a unique sacramental presence of God when his people gather. Individualism dies in the book of Acts.

However, a theology of the church does not stop there in Acts. The Spirit tears down walls of hostility as the message of Jesus goes from Jerusalem to the wider region and finally to the ends of the earth. The Father's plan, Jesus's body, and the Spirit's work create a diverse group of Jesus followers: men and women, rich and poor, slave and free, barbarian and educated, leaders and followers, dark skin and light skin. A renewal in the church will look less segregated and more integrated. A renewal in the church will look more like every tongue from every nation coming together to worship the cross-cultural King.

Seventh, we observed how the church was to be a witness to the ends of the earth. The spread of the fame of Jesus's name is not an option. It is not to be put on the list of things to do after other things are accomplished. Mission is essential to ministry and practice. It is not an accessory to the church but the lens through which we view everything. As Christopher Wright has argued, mission is *not* one of a hundred different biblical themes that we might explore.[6] Nor does it merely refer to overseas ministry. The whole Bible can be put under the banner of mission, and is even the product of that mission. It is the mission of God to confront us with the reality of himself (his glory). He does so by revealing himself in the story we find in the Scriptures. In one sense, this whole text is a mission text. He enacts his mission and furthers his mission specifically through his people. We have a God of mission, we are a people of mission, and we have an arena of mission.

Chrysostom ends his homilies on Acts pointing both to the work of the triune God and the imitation of Paul:

> Let us emulate Paul, and imitate that noble, that adamantine soul: that advancing in the steps of his life, we may be enabled to sail the sea of this present life, and to come unto the haven wherein are no waves, and attain unto the good things promised to them that love Him, through the grace and mercy of our Lord Jesus Christ, with Whom the Father and the Holy Ghost together be glory, might, honor, now and ever, world without end. Amen.[7]

---

6 Christopher J. H. Wright, *The Mission of God: Unlocking the Bible's Grand Narrative*, repr. ed. (Downers Grove, IL: IVP Academic, 2018).

7 Chrysostom, Homily 55 on Acts, in *NPNF*, Series 1, vol. 11, ed. Philip Schaff (Grand Rapids, MI: Eerdmans, 1925), 328.

The book of Acts shows that we live "between the times," and our job here on earth is to tell forth the triune God who has revealed himself in the face of Jesus Christ. As the angels instructed the disciples in Acts, stop looking into heaven. We have work to do on earth.

Every piece of the Christian canon, including Acts, imparts a theology. This theology in Acts is logically and narratively ordered. Luke wrote an orderly account of events to provide certainty to his readers and future readers (Luke 1:3–4).

The foundations of the ancient church provide the footings for the renewal of the modern church.

Recommended Resources

Commentaries

Barnes, Albert. *Notes Explanatory and Practical on the Acts of the Apostles.* New York: Harper, 1851.

Bock, Darrell L. *Acts.* Baker Exegetical Commentary on the New Testament. Grand Rapids, MI: Baker Academic, 2007.

Dunn, James D. G. *The Acts of the Apostles.* Grand Rapids, MI: Eerdmans, 1996.

Erasmus, Desiderius. *Paraphrase on Acts.* Translated by Robert D. Sider. Collected Works of Erasmus 50. Toronto: University of Toronto Press, 1995.

Gaventa, Beverly R. *Acts.* Abingdon New Testament Commentaries. Nashville, TN: Abingdon, 2003.

Jennings, Willie James. *Acts: A Theological Commentary on the Bible.* Louisville, KY: Westminster John Knox, 2017.

Marshall, I. Howard. *The Acts of the Apostles: An Introduction and Commentary.* Grand Rapids, MI: Eerdmans, 1980.

Martin, Francis, ed. *Acts.* Ancient Christian Commentary Series. Downers Grove, IL: InterVarsity, 2006.

Moore, Mark E. *Acts.* The College Press NIV Commentary. Joplin, MO: College Press, 2011.

Parsons, Mikeal C. *Acts.* Paideia. Grand Rapids, MI: Baker Academic, 2008.

Peterson, David G. *The Acts of the Apostles.* Pillar New Testament Commentary. Grand Rapids, MI: Eerdmans, 2009.

Schreiner, Patrick. *Acts*. Christian Standard Commentary. Nashville, TN: Holman, 2022.

Stott, John. *The Spirit, the Church and the World: The Message of Acts*. Downers Grove, IL: Intervarsity, 1990.

Spencer, F. Scott. *Journeying through Acts: A Literary-Cultural Reading*. Sheffield: Sheffield Academic, 1997.

Tannehill, Robert C. *The Narrative Unity of Luke-Acts: A Literary Interpretation*, vol. 2, *The Acts of the Apostles*. Philadelphia, PA: Fortress, 1990.

Witherington, Ben. *The Acts of the Apostles: A Socio-Rhetorical Commentary*. Grand Rapids, MI: Eerdmans, 1998.

Theologies

Anderson, Kevin L. *But God Raised Him from the Dead: The Theology of Jesus's Resurrection in Luke-Acts*. Eugene, OR: Wipf & Stock, 2007.

Beale, G. K. *The Temple and the Church's Mission*. New Studies in Biblical Theology 17. Downers Grove, IL: IVP Academic, 2004.

Beers, Holly. *The Followers of Jesus as the "Servant": Luke's Model from Isaiah for the Disciples in Luke-Acts*. London: Bloomsbury T&T Clark, 2016.

Bock, Darrell L. *A Theology of Luke and Acts: God's Promised Program, Realized for All Nations*. Edited by Andreas J. Köstenberger. Grand Rapids, MI: Zondervan, 2012.

Crowe, Brandon D. *The Hope of Israel: The Resurrection of Christ in the Acts of the Apostles*. Grand Rapids, MI: Baker Academic, 2020.

Cunningham, Scott. *Through Many Tribulations: The Theology of Persecution in Luke-Acts*. Journal for the Study of the New Testament Supplement Series 142. Sheffield, UK: Sheffield Academic, 1997.

Esler, Philip Francis. *Community and Gospel in Luke-Acts*. Cambridge: Cambridge University Press, 1987.

Farrow, Douglas. *Ascension and Ecclesia: On the Significance of the Doctrine of the Ascension for Ecclesiology and Christian Cosmology*. Grand Rapids, MI: Eerdmans, 1999.

Garrett, Susan. *The Demise of the Devil: Magic and the Demonic in Luke's Writings*. Minneapolis, MN: Fortress, 1989.

Goulder, M. D. *Type and History in Acts*. London: SPCK, 1964.

Jipp, Joshua. *Reading Acts*. Cascade Companions. Eugene, OR: Cascade Books, 2018.

Johnson, Dennis E. *The Message of Acts in the History of Redemption*. Phillipsburg, NJ: P&R, 1997.

Marshall, I. Howard, and David Peterson, eds. *Witness to the Gospel: The Theology of Acts*. Grand Rapids, MI: Eerdmans, 1998.

Orr, Peter. *Exalted Above the Heavens: The Risen and Ascended Christ*. New Studies in Biblical Theology 47. Downers Grove, IL: IVP Academic, 2019.

Padilla, Osvaldo. *The Acts of the Apostles: Interpretation, History and Theology*. Downers Grove: IVP Academic, 2016.

Padilla, Osvaldo. *The Speeches of Outsiders in Acts: Poetics, Theology, and Historiography*. Society for New Testament Studies Monograph Series 144. Cambridge: Cambridge University Press, 2008.

Pao, David W. *Acts and the Isaianic New Exodus*. Eugene, OR: Wipf & Stock, 2016.

Rowe, C. Kavin. *World Upside Down: Reading Acts in the Graeco-Roman Age*. Oxford: Oxford University Press, 2010.

Schreiner, Patrick. *The Ascension of Christ: Recovering a Neglected Doctrine*. Bellingham, WA: Lexham, 2020.

Sleeman, Matthew. *Geography and the Ascension Narrative in Acts*. Cambridge: Cambridge University Press, 2009.

Squires, John T. *The Plan of God in Luke-Acts*. Cambridge; New York: Cambridge University Press, 1993.

Thompson, Alan. *The Acts of the Risen Lord Jesus: Luke's Account of God's Unfolding Plan*. New Studies in Biblical Theology 27. Downers Grove, IL: InterVarsity, 2011.

Turner, Max. *Power from on High: The Spirit in Israel's Restoration and Witness in Luke-Acts*. Sheffield: Sheffield Academic, 1996.

Articles

Bird, Michael F. "The Unity of Luke-Acts in Recent Discussion." *Journal for the Study of the New Testament* 29, no. 4 (2007): 425–48.

Blomberg, Craig L. "The Law in Luke-Acts." *Journal for the Study of the New Testament* 7, no. 22 (1984): 53–80.

Carter, Warren. "Aquatic Display: Navigating the Roman Imperial World in Acts 27." *New Testament Studies* 62, no. 1 (2016): 79–96.

Gaventa, Beverly Roberts. "Toward a Theology of Acts: Reading and Re-reading." *Interpretation* 42, no. 2 (1988): 146–57.

Gilbert, Gary. "The List of Nations in Acts 2: Roman Propaganda and the Lukan Response." *Journal of Biblical Literature* 121, no. 3 (2002): 497–529.

Le Donne, Anthony. "The Improper Temple Offering of Ananias and Sapphira." *New Testament Studies* 59, no. 3 (2013): 346–64.

Jipp, Joshua. "Hospitable Barbarians: Luke's Ethnic Reasoning in Acts 28:1–10." *The Journal of Theological Studies* 68, no. 1 (2017): 23–45.

Jipp, Joshua. "Paul's Areopagus Speech of Acts 17:16–34 as Both Critique and Propaganda." *Journal of Biblical Literature* 131, no. 3 (2012): 567–88.

Rowe, Kavin. "The Grammar of Life: The Areopagus Speech and Pagan Tradition." *New Testament Studies* 57, no. 1 (2011): 31–50.

Rowe, C. Kavin. "Luke-Acts and the Imperial Cult: A Way Through the Conundrum?" *Journal for the Study of the New Testament* 27, no. 3 (2005): 279–300.

Schreiner, Patrick. "Evaluating the Validity of the 'Three Missionary Journeys' Structuring Motif in Acts." *The Journal of the Evangelical Theological Society* 63, no. 3 (2020): 505–16.

General Index

Scripture Index

Also Available in the New Testament Theology Series

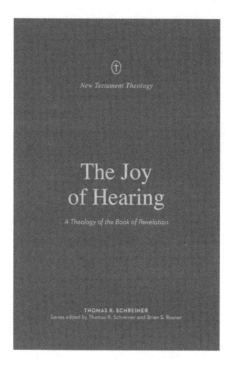

Edited by Thomas R. Schreiner and Brian S. Rosner, this series presents clear, scholarly overviews of the main theological themes of each book of the New Testament, examining what they reveal about God, Christ, and how they connect to the overarching biblical narrative.

For more information, visit **crossway.org**.